# DARTMOOR STONE

# DARTMOOR STONE

## STEPHEN H. WOODS

Published by Devon Books in association with the
Dartmoor National Park Authority

First published in Great Britain in 1988 by Devon Books

ISBN: 0 86114 841 X (cased edition)
0 86114 843 6 (limp edition)

**British Library Cataloguing-in-Publication Data**
Woods, Stephen
    Dartmoor stone.
    1. Devon, Dartmoor. Materials. Granite
    to 1988
    I. Title
    620.1′32′0942353

*Dartmoor Stone* is published by Devon Books in association with the Dartmoor National Park Authority, Parke, Bovey Tracey TQ13 9JQ

Special thanks to John Weir.

Typeset in Great Britain by P&M Typesetting, Exeter
Monochrome reproduction by Peninsular Repro Services Ltd, Exeter

Printed and bound in Great Britain by A. Wheaton & Co. Ltd

DEVON BOOKS

Official Publisher to Devon County Council

An imprint of Wheaton Publishers Ltd.
A Member of Maxwell Pergamon Publishing Corporation plc

Wheaton Publishers Ltd
Hennock Road, Marsh Barton, Exeter, Devon EX2 8RP
Tel: 0392 74121; Telex 42794 (WHEATN G)

SALES

Direct sales enquiries to Devon Books at the address above.

# FOREWORD

'Landscape is the function of structure, process and time' said one William Davies a long time ago. For a National Park Officer who taught Davies' subject for half his working life, that text is reinvoked by this book. It demonstrates the universality of its truth in ways Davies never contemplated, and exemplifies what British National Parks are all about. Granite and all its characteristics are the structure, man's energy, application and ingenuity are the process, and the timespan is a crescendo from ancient, deep emplacement, through exposure to the air, to human manipulation.

No other National Park is so dominated by a single type of rock, either naturally or culturally. Dartmoor and granite are inseparable, to many synonymous. Hence Stephen Woods' title. These photographs celebrate granite, and the love and care and work of Dartmoor people over five thousand years. They also register one man's worship, through his own skill, of all that other labour.

The care and maintenance of this great granite cathedral of space and scenic detail, decorated by men with menhirs and stone rows, with walls and barns, with houses and churches, falls now to a National Park Authority, and a growing corps of masons, wallers and farmers prompted by it. It is our earnest hope that this book will give pleasure to many, and explain, in passing, the motivation for conserving the stone, the artefact and the skills.

IAN MERCER
DARTMOOR NATIONAL PARK OFFICER

# CONTENTS

To my family

# ACKNOWLEDGEMENTS

Three ladies have had a great influence on my life: Edith French of Dockwell, who when I was a boy taught me a love of the countryside, she teased me continuously, but I always went back for more; Iris Woods, my mother whose interest and knowledge of Dartmoor's history and people far exceeds mine, and who did so much research for me; Valerie Woods, my wife, who suffered my enthusiasm and often single-mindedness, which can be summed up in my daughter's words, 'not another standing stone!', as I deviously devised our walks. I am indebted to her for transcribing my scribble into legible type, not once but several times as I strove to get my thoughts together.

I must also record the pleasure given to me by our children, Robert, Christopher, Karen and Andrew, who vied with each other to accompany me on my early morning walks. Only I and they know where they are hidden in my photographs.

I am indebted to a host of others, who added to my knowledge, many I have never met, but who courteously answered my letters: Anthony Beard; Bessie Beard (deceased); Gwen Beard; Mark Beeson; Dave and Kath Brewer; Jack Brown (deceased); Mr Canon (deceased); Miss Cave-Penney (deceased); Andrew Fleming; Hermon French (deceased); Elizabeth Gawne; Tom Greeves; Mary Hamlyn (deceased); Bob Haynes; Katherine Longley (for translations); Susan Pearce; Iris Pulley Clark; Mrs W.G. Clarke; Lady Sayer; J. Somers Cocks; the Vicars of Widecombe – the Reverend Brown and Reverend Bulley; Mr and Mrs Westwood; Freda Wilkinson; my father, Albert Woods (deceased); my brothers John Woods (deceased), and Rollo Woods.

And I thank the people of the Moor whose names I do not know, like the moorman farmer who was feeding extra minerals to his cattle. We stood beside May's House and discussed the excellence of the grass, while watching his wife dismount and make her way deep into the mire to check a cow and its small calf. It was not yet 7a.m. and I wonder how many visitors realise they would do this daily, no matter what the weather, while their charges were on the Moor.

There are an army of Librarians and Archivists who sort out my problems, advise and cater to my needs; I thank you all.

STEPHEN WOODS
PORTCHESTER
HANTS
JULY 1988

BEARDOWN MAN
(sx 596 797)

This standing stone, more commonly known locally as a menhir, varies in
shape and stature depending from which side it is viewed. Compare this to
another view in chapter 2.

# INTRODUCTION

I took up photography as the substance of my career in 1947, so this book has evolved over a great many years. It started out as a collection of indiscriminate snapshots taken on so many joyful walks on the moors, or strolls along the river bank. First with my parents and brothers, then with my wife Valerie, and later our children.

For those interested in photography, my first camera was a Zeiss Kolibri, followed by a Super Ikonta, both now collectors' pieces. For many years I used a Canon 35mm and have now graduated to a Hasselblad. The photographs are straightforward record shots, which often presents problems with inscribed stones. I have resisted temptation to outline with chalk, and would dearly have liked to use a wire brush on occasion to remove lichens. Since my friend Dave Brewer went into print about boundary stones, I have noticed an increase in the uses of substances to infill letters, even in one case paint!

Evolution is part of the human character, and the need for a sense of purpose made me decide on a theme – 'Man's use of granite on Dartmoor', a subject which did not alter one jot what I was already doing, but it added research. I needed to know how many different ways granite had been utilized over the centuries, and where the best examples were to be found.

Local libraries provide a fund of knowledge and they are able to find information which at times seems tantalisingly out of reach. In seeking information I have followed in William Borlase's steps which he concisely stated in the preface to his *Antiquities of Cornwall*. 'I have neither neglected the learned nor unlearned; but I have gathered what plain truths I found in each, and endeavoured to illustrate my subject with both; but never copied either that I can recollect, without taking care that every Reader should know it.'

I have of course spoken to local people (which I never found easy), and have passed a 'site' several times before I could pluck up courage to knock and ask my questions. Only once was I refused the opportunity to take my photographs and that was only because my timing was totally inappropriate. In fact I found it very stimulating that so many 'workers' would down tools and spend time talking and showing me around. Personal contact is very rewarding.

Readers are reminded, however, that many of the sites and artefacts described in this work are on private property where permission must be sought before attempting access.

The tin industry is about to pass beyond living memory. Of those who went down a mine while it was still working, probably less than a score are still living. I am fortunate that my mother, Iris Woods, now ninety years old, did so in 1913. She, with a friend and my grandfather, walked up the Redwater Valley past the Golden Dagger mine, which showed no signs of life, to the Birch Tor Vitifer mine. My mother recalls her father saying 'Would you like to go into the mine'?

*'Of course we said yes, and made our way to the opening of a narrow tunnel which was the entrance. The walls were solid granite with wooden supports here and there. A small stream ran down the path. A short distance inside a man met us, and agreed to show us*

*the workings. He produced three candles from his pocket, lighted them, and handed them to us to carry. As we went forward the darkness increased till we could see nothing except by the glimmer of our candles. It was evident that the water dripping from the roof and down the walls was the source of the stream. When we reached the point where the entrance was only a tiny distant gleam of light, we came to a wooden ladder fastened against the wall leading through a hole in the roof to the place where work was going on, for we could hear the sound of hammering. Our guide had produced three pairs of large wellington boots which we put on over our shoes. We were then required to climb the ladder. Every time I lifted my foot, the boot dropped off and it was obvious that I should never be able to mount the ladder. So it was decided that I should wait at the bottom while the others went up, my father first, then my friend, and then the miner. I was left in the darkness, made worse rather than better by my single candle. Water ran down the walls and dripped from the tunnel roof, threatening to drown the candle, and I had no matches. Small pieces of rock came rattling down from the roof, now and then quite large pieces descended.*

*I could neither see nor hear anything of my companions. Drips fell on my head and down my neck, and I was exceedingly thankful when boots began to descend.*

*There had been nothing much to see above, only a narrow gallery from which bits of tin stone were being chiselled off.'*

The hammering was really the death knell of over seven hundred years of endeavour. My first film contained some shots of this mine, the 'dry' with its chimney still standing. Alas some vandal pushed it over and a bare outline is all that remains today.

This book contains a selection of my efforts to record a visual history of the Dartmoor people over a period of six thousand years, an impossible task for this small book. I have taken four or five thousand negatives, edited to about a thousand prints in my albums, cut to some 400 for this volume. The list of objects I hope one day to photograph seems never to get any shorter.

I have written a brief outline to accompany the photographs in order to provide a background to an historical period, the growth and decline of an industry, or the evolution of an individual subject. I hope the reader will enjoy this treatise on a material, *Dartmoor Stone.*

STEPHEN WOODS
1988

THE LONGSTONE
(sx 660 857)

This final stone of a row, mentioned as a boundary point in the 1240 perambulation, is also a bound stone, engraved with the letters DC (Duchy of Cornwall), C (Chagford), GP (Gidleigh Parish).

SHOVEL DOWN
(sx 660 859)

In this view of the north flank of Shovel Down are three stone rows. One,
headed by fourfold retaining circles, leads down to Batworthy corner. This
must have been an area of great significance to the prehistoric people.

BENNETT'S CROSS
(sx 680 817)

The old cross marks one of the ancient packhorse tracks across the moor.
Being there 'tyme out of mind' it was used as a parish bound stone, a bound
for the Birch Tor Vitifer mine, and for Headland Warren, here denoted by
the letters W.B.

POWDERMILLS
(sx 627 774)

This site is of great industrial archaeological interest for so much of the
works remain. Here rock powder (gunpowder) was produced, used both in
mines and quarries.

BIRCH TOR VITIFER MINE
(sx 682 809)

A view of the Dry, where the miners ending their shifts would change and
dry their clothes. The walk up from the Golden Dagger mine in winter
soaked to the skin, must have been an unpleasant experience.
This is one of the first photographs taken by the author, in 1948.

*. . . Time destroys*
*His statues, and his columns, and his domes,*
*Flings his triumphant arches to the ground,*
*And gnaws the names of heroes and of kings,*
*E'en from the marble tablet . . .*
*. . . while here, unhurt –*
*Wed almost to eternity – secure*
*In their own strength, proud baffling all the rage*
*Of the defeated elements, and all*
*The ceaseless injuries of time – remain*
*The columns of the wilderness.*

N T Carrington,
*Dartmoor a Descriptive Poem, 1826*

# PROLOGUE

*'....the inhabitants of a civilised country are much governed in their occupation, all other things being equal, by the geological structure of that country....'*
HENRY T DE LA BECHE, 1839

All landscapes begin with rock. The bulk of Dartmoor comprises one rock type – granite. It occurs as a single block, with the exception of two small outcrops south of Lee Moor, and extends over some 241 square miles. This grey rock has shaped the Dartmoor countryside, an elevated region rising to 2038ft (621m) above sea level. On this surface people have lived, farmed, worked stone and buried their dead for thousands of years; they continue to do so. Their activities have left their mark on the ground, and the evidence – stone walls, earth-covered mounds and banks, stones set upright – is all around. Withstanding wind and rain, the tenacity of these remains lies in the lasting quality of granite.

The word granite (from the Italian *granito*, meaning grained, granular) first came into somewhat limited use in our vocabulary in the eighteenth century. Marshall, writing in 1796, refers to 'Moorstone or Quartzose Granite' as being found plentifully on Dartmoor. Henry T de la Beche in his *Report of the Geology of Cornwall, Devon and West Somerset* (1839), reminds us that a substance so easily distinguished as granite did not escape the earliest geological researches in Devon and Cornwall. Indeed, the isolated character of the main granitic masses of south-western England was pointed out by William Smith in his *Geological Map of England and Wales* (1815) and in more detail in Greenough's map of 1819.

Granite is a plutonic rock beginning its life as molten material (magma), rising from great depth in the Earth. As magma rises it intrudes the cold rocks of the upper crust and cools slowly. The slower it cools the bigger the crystals of its main constituents: in granite's case quartz, felspars and micas. Other minerals are locally abundant. The rock surface now seen is a mosaic of interlocking crystals and here, in part, lies its strength. Its relatively high content of quartz – an extremely stable mineral and a substance harder than steel – adds significantly to its defiance to the elements.

Some 280–395 million years ago – from the Devonian to the late Carboniferous periods – the area in which Dartmoor's present rocks were formed was part of a large sea floor. Sediments were being deposited on it mainly by rivers flowing down from mountains to the north. These sediments are today represented around Dartmoor's granite mass by slates, shales, mudstones, sandstones, limestones, cherts and conglomerates. Some 290 million years ago these sediments were subject to intense crustal pressure from the north and south in a major mountain building episode. They were crumpled to form a mountain chain – the Cornubians. Into the roots of these mountains magma welled up and cooled to form granite.

As the granite cooled, it and the immediately surrounding country rocks were affected in places by super-heated gases and vapours which rose through the magma into the many fissures. These vapours converted felspars to kaolinite, and also cooled and crystallised to form veins and lodes containing a variety of metalliferous minerals including tin, copper, lead, silver and zinc. In particular tin ore – cassiterite – occurred in abundance.

The Cornubian Mountains no longer exist. They were eroded away during the following Permian and Triassic Periods and were submerged under a shallow sea. Other rocks were deposited over their stumps during the Cretaceous Period (65–110 million years ago). By about 65 million years ago these had been eroded away in their turn and the granite was exposed to the air for the first time.

Rivers on this new landscape were flowing eastward in the main and carried granite pebbles and kaolin into east Dorset. Quite soon the earth movements which elsewhere formed the Alps, the Rockies and the Andes, uplifted what is now south-west England and tilted it southward. A major fracture from Torquay to the Pembrokeshire coast, passing through the eastern edge of the granite, occurred at the same time. A tropical climate prevailed whose warm, acid rain attacked the granite domes protruding through the forest cover and fed the new rivers which now were tempted southward. This was how the Dartmoor upland was born.

The initial cooling, and the removal of the original overlying rock, caused the characteristic cracks and fissures in the granite which geologists and quarrymen call joints. These joints – well seen in all exposed granite – were the initial pathways for the warm weak acids of the tropical rain forest, being widened by chemical attack, largely on the felspar crystals. The resultant clay, loosened quartz and mica crystals were sluiced out and deposited in the surrounding

The combination of dense fractures and exposed locations, meant that granite was easily exploited by weathering and erosive agencies.

landscape, is now found between Bovey Tracey and Newton Abbot, and at Meeth and Petrockstowe. More than sixty million years later (some 10000–600000 years ago) arctic conditions exploited the joints again. Constant freezing and thawing of water in them levered away block after block to narrow down hilltops, spur ends, and the lips of valley sides, leaving the tors for which Dartmoor is so well known. Below them lie the boulder fields called 'clitters' and the sheets of gravel produced by the same mechanical means. The clitter, dense below the tors and scattered on gentler slopes, is the 'moorstone' which man has put to use in so many ways.

In the 1820s a Mr Cottle considered moorstone as an encumbrance saying that 'One great impediment ... to the cultivation of Dartmoor will arise from the immense number of large stones, with which nearly the whole surface of the land is closely covered. To remove them, wholly, or to gather them into heaps ... would be almost impracticable. The thought occurred to me on the spot that the most frugal and effectual way to get rid of these stones would be by digging deep holes immediately adjoining, and then by burying them'. Fortunately his plan was never adopted.

Throughout the evolution of civilization we have steadily broadened our use of the rock, mineral and energy resources of the Earth. The potential of Dartmoor's freely occurring surface granite was recognized first by prehistoric peoples for the building of chambered tombs some 5000 years ago. Soon after, ritualistic monuments such as menhirs, stone circles and rows, were raised. Moorstone was also cropped for prehistoric boundaries and for the foundations of homes.

Human ingenuity provided solutions to questions of 'How to do and move this?' and 'How to use that?' At first lack of appropriate splitting tools meant that the best use was made of the stone as it was. The right to take stone from the moor for 'domestic' use, by commoners, has its origins in time obscure, and by the Norman Conquest some stone had been cut and dressed from surface blocks. Since then granite has been cut and transported by the ton as rural engineers put the moorstone to a variety of uses.

By medieval times churches, houses and farm outbuildings were being built of cut and dressed stone. Tinners used the stone in the construction of blowing houses and adapted it for the processing of tin ore – in crushing stamps, in furnace walls and for mortars and mouldstones. The enclosure of agricultural land was aided by the abundance of available moorstone, which had to be cleared anyway, for use in walls and hedgebanks, or as gateposts and stiles. It was also adopted for a range of farm and domestic equipment such as cider and cheese presses, querns, troughs and rollers. Moorstone was shaped into wayside crosses and, because it yielded large slabs of sound stone, it was used to span rivers, streams and leats.

Evidence of stone cutting on the moor is prolific. Prehistoric monuments and even the tors themselves failed to escape the attention of later exploiters. At Merrivale, on Long Ash Common, somewhere around 1860, a farmer cut a gatepost out of a slab forming a cover to a kistvaen. Such activities largely went unrecorded but a recycling process on a large scale must have taken place.

The quarrying of Dartmoor granite first began in the 1780s. At this time trans-moorland roads were being built and Princetown, as a settlement, was founded. A great deal of stone was quarried from nearby Foggintor for the construction of houses and, soon after, for the building of Princetown Prison and church. The Plymouth and Dartmoor Railway was opened in 1823 and this facilitated the development of quarries in the Princetown area. Further markets could then be developed and considerable quantities of granite were being exported for use in London and elsewhere. The exploitation of granite had shifted from the vernacular to the whims of external commercialism:

*... see, the sail*
*Of Commerce flitters near, till patient skill*
*And dauntless toil prepare the polish'd cubes*
*Immense, that soon shall form the proudest domes*
*Of yonder proud metropolis!*

N T Carrington, 1826

Two views of the quarry at Princetown Prison, taken in about 1880. The left hand picture shows prisoners wearing goggles to protect their eyes as they break up granite for roadstone.

The opening of New London Bridge, 1837.

Bench quarrying, Merrivale. Thermal lances cut horizontal through–
channels to allow controlled blasting. Charges are placed into vertical holes
and the explosion shifts the bench of its bed for further cutting.

Indeed, the first railway in Devon was constructed to serve a granite quarry at Haytor. This railway, opened in 1820, ran for almost ten miles and was itself made of granite. It linked a canal which enabled the transport of granite to the Teign estuary and the English Channel, and thence to London. In 1825 Haytor granite was used for the rebuilding of the new London Bridge.

Elsewhere, other quarries were opened up, such as at Heckwood in the Walkham Valley from which stone was used for the Plymouth Breakwater.

Smaller quarries were also founded for supplying specific local needs. On the southern lower slopes of Western Beacon, stone was quarried for the construction of the railway viaducts at Ivybridge and Cornwood, and granite from a quarry near Burrator Reservoir was used in the construction of the dam.

Illicit taking, and abuse of licenses to quarry granite bedrock or to remove moorstone, was commonplace. In some instances the tors themselves were physically assaulted. In about 1847 protection limits around Pew Tor and Staple Tor had to be created by the Duchy of Cornwall – this action was one of the first deliberate conservation measures taken to protect vital elements in the Dartmoor landscape.

Throughout the nineteenth and into the twentieth century a fluctuating but often flourishing quarry industry developed. Competition from Cornish and overseas quarries proved too great and today only one quarry, at Merrivale, is still in commercial operation.

Merrivale Quarry was opened in 1875 by William Duke and it was then known as Tor Quarry. Removed and worked stone was taken by road-tractor steam engines to the railway at Tavistock. Today, the quarry provides sixteen fulltime jobs and is worked by Natural Stone Products, a subsidiary of Tarmac. Main uses of the granite product are for building fabrication and street kerbing. The most modern extraction and processing systems are used – thermal lances allow accurate cutting at the quarry face and computerized and fully automated saws ensure millimetre accuracy. The workforce not only handles indigenous Dartmoor granite – a wide selection of granites quarried in Scandinavia, India, South Africa and the Americas is also processed for specific architectural needs. Recently the quarry has handled contracts involving the Falklands Memorial, the paving of Trafalgar Square and the refurbishing of Tower Bridge. And, some 160 years after Haytor granite was shipped for the building of a New London Bridge, that granite was returned to Dartmoor to Merrivale Quarry – here it was cut into four-inch face slabs and then shipped to Arizona to face a concrete-built replica sitting in a leisure park.

Paradoxically, in some areas of Dartmoor the use of granite has heightened a sense of wilderness. The isolated menhir echoes timelessness, and the deserted quarry amplifies our temporariness. Writing in the 1930s Eden Phillpotts described the abandoned Haytor Quarry and the power of nature to reclaim:

Haytor Quarry, 1829.

*The quarry lies like a gash in the slopes of the hills. To the dizzy edges of it creep heather and the bracken; beneath, upon its precipices, a stout rowan or two rise, and everywhere Nature has fought and laboured to hide this wound driven so deep into her mountainside by man. A cicatrix of moss and fern and many grasses conceal the scars of pick and gunpowder; time has weathered the harsh edges of the riven stone; the depths of the quarry are covered by pools of clear water ... one may drink from this cup all the mystery that fills a deserted theatre of man's work and feel that loneliness which only human ruins tell ...*

The innate quality of granite is that it rarely loses its 'naturalness' whatever human use it takes, and a harmony between our species and nature is achieved – a far cry from the predominantly synthetic world of today. That made of granite has been born out of the land, not inflicted upon it. Its manmade contributions to the landscape are recognized by the National Park Authority – it employs a stonemason and relies on local skills to maintain the detail. It utilises the enduring stone to restore river banks and other areas where countless numbers of feet have eroded the surface; it supports the maintenance of walls and hedgebanks and aids the conservation of archaeological sites and historical buildings.

Blocks of granite are raised from the quarry at Merrivale and are then sliced
by computer-controlled blocksaws. Both block and blade are constantly
cooled by water. The saws – up to 2.5–3 metres in diameter – consist of
diamond tips bedded into cobalt.

Fully automated secondary saws help to ensure unsurpassed accuracy.

Stonemasons use pneumatic tools and grinders and polishers to clean up rough edges.

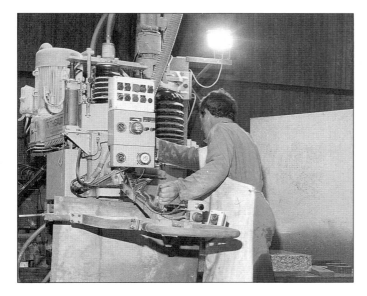

A range of six alternative finishes – polished, honed, flame-textured, fine axed, dolly pointed and rough punched – is achieved using computer-controlled equipment for polishing and texturing.

A finished product, part of a complex architectural design, destined for Salford. 'If that's the shape they want then that's the shape they'll get' – Mr Metters, Foreman, Merrivale Quarry.

The approach to Widecombe Village sign, badly eroded by thousands of visitors annually, has been repaired and paved with granite setts to prevent similar damage in the future. The National Park Authority undertook the work with the assistance of the Parish Council.

The photographs in this book provide reminders of a sometimes harsh though simple way of life with ritualistic and religious, agricultural, industrial and domestic associations. The supporting captions provide a factual platform for their interpretation but the photographs also stand alone. They reveal the pattern of light on the rock and all are an artistic impression of texture and natural and human sculpture.

The dimension of Dartmoor spans from individual crystals that make up the rock itself through a myriad of natural and human detail to sharp and blurred horizons. It is a huge beauty, one in which our roots are deeply engraved in the rock. Granite gives a sense of place, the human use the genius of place. Invariably we make an indelible imprint on the land but, as portrayed in these pages, this need not be despoliation. We of the present and those of the future should safeguard an inheritance that has for so long survived.

JOHN WEIR

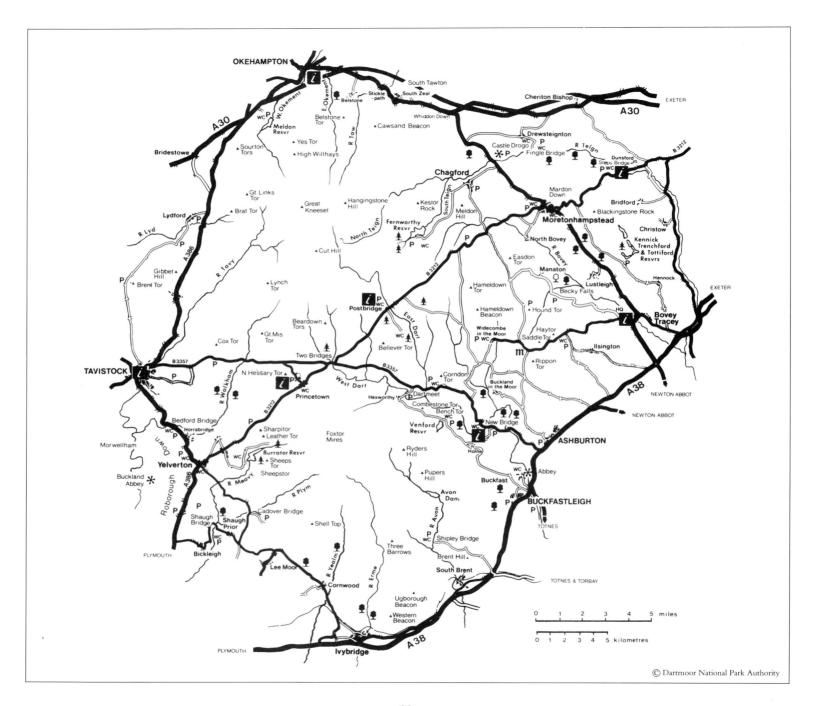

OKEHAMPTON

EXETER

A30

Cheriton Bishop

South Tawton
South Zeal

A30

Bridestowe

Belstone
Stickle
path

Belstone
Tor

Whiddon Down

Drewsteignton

Castle Drogo

Fingle Bridge

R Teign

Dunsford
Steps Bridge

B3212

Meldon
Resvr

Sourton
Tors

Yes Tor

High Willhays

Cawsand Beacon

W Okement

E Okement

R Taw

Chagford

Mardon
Down

Bridford

Blackingstone Rock

Christow

Kennick
Trenchford
& Tottiford
Resvrs

Hennock

EXETER

Lydford

R Lyd

Gt. Links
Tor

Brat Tor

Great
Kneeset

Hangingstone
Hill

Kestor
Rock

South Teign

Meldon
Hill

Moretonhampstead

North Bovey

North Teign

Fernworthy
Resvr

R Bovey

Easdon
Tor

Manaton

Lustleigh

Becky Falls

Gibbet
Hill

Brent Tor

R Tavy

Cut Hill

Lynch
Tor

Hameldown
Tor

Hameldown
Beacon

Hound Tor

Haytor
Saddle Tor

Bovey
Tracey

HQ

Cox Tor

Gt. Mis
Tor

Beardown
Tors

Postbridge

East Dart

Believer Tor

Widecombe
in the Moor

Ilsington

Tavistock

B3357

Two Bridges

B3357

Rippon
Tor

N.Hessary Tor

West Dart

Corndon
Tor

A38

NEWTON ABBOT

Princetown

B3212

Dartmeet

Hexworthy

Combestone Tor

Buckland
in the Moor

NEWTON ABBOT

R Walkham

Bedford Bridge

Horrabridge

Sharpitor
Leather Tor

Foxtor
Mires

Bench Tor

New Bridge

Venford
Resvr

Holne

ASHBURTON

Morwellham

Burrator Resvr

Sheeps
Tor

Sheepstor

Ryders
Hill

Abbey

Yelverton

Buckland
Abbey

Roborough Down

A386

R Meavy

Cadover Bridge

R Plym

Pupers
Hill

Avon
Dam

Buckfast

BUCKFASTLEIGH

TOTNES

Shaugh
Bridge

Shaugh
Prior

Shell Top

R Avon

Shipley Bridge

PLYMOUTH

Bickleigh

Lee Moor

R Yealm

Three
Barrows

Brent Hill

TOTNES & TORBAY

Cornwood

R Erme

Ugborough
Beacon

Western
Beacon

South Brent

A38

PLYMOUTH

Ivybridge

0 1 2 3 4 5 miles

0 1 2 3 4 5 kilometres

© Dartmoor National Park Authority

30

# 1
# IN THE
# BEGINNING

In the beginning... or about three to four hundred million years ago, the area now known as Dartmoor was divided in two, made up of Devonian sediments in the south and Carboniferous deposits to the north, the whole being covered by a warm sea.

A period of upheaval and folding was followed some 290 million years ago by the upsurge of molten matter which pushed apart the Devonian and Carboniferous rocks and exuded outwards both to the north and south. This material cooled to form granite, composed of quartz, mica and felspar. In the ensuing millennia the surface was eroded or decomposed to form growan, the underlying surface of the moor, with hard cores of granite being laid bare to form the characteristic tors of today.

The hot granite caused changes to the existing rocks, forming shales, grits, cherts and limestones. Known as the metamorphic aureole, this comprises a narrow band of mineral rich rocks surrounding the granite mass of today's Dartmoor.

As the granite cooled it cracked producing horizontal and vertical joints. The horizontal joints occur according to the lie of the land; that is to say the hilltop tor joints tend to be horizontal whereas valley-side outcrops tend to follow the slope of the land. Other substances infiltrated into the joints such as tourmaline, a black deposit which seems to cling to the granite, and mineralised liquids and gases such as iron, lead, copper and tin.

Decomposition also occurred from below; hot liquids played on the underside of the granite breaking down the felspar to form kaolin. This has been mined at several points on the moor, leaving the quartz and mica to form disfiguring waste tips.

When the Alps were formed, Dartmoor was tilted towards the south by an upheaval, greatest in the north-west. The rivers that were already set in the landscape had their impetus changed. This is seen by the length of the Dart's northern tributaries compared to those on its south bank. The Plym, Yealm, Erme and Avon were also able to reach further into the moor.

Dartmoor became an island during the Ice Ages, the water reaching the 690 foot contour. The mechanical action of frost during these periods is amply demonstrated by the clitter scattered down the valley sides.

With the defrosting of the land, and as the temperature rose at the end of the final Ice Age, trees and shrubs began to flourish. First pine and birch, followed by alder, oak and hazel, covered most of Dartmoor's surface, though on the highest lands open spaces are very likely to have always existed.

Reindeer moved north with the retreating ice and their territory was taken by the red deer, which would survive today but for man's unforgiving hand.

It was man who enlarged and created the open space of today's moorland, clearing the forests until only the valleys of the major rivers could protect those trees that remained, and most of those had to eke out their lives among the clitter of the valley sides. Heavy grazing of the moor by sheep and cattle in historic times continued and maintained the process of clearance. The tinners also contributed by prospecting for tin in the valley bottoms.

By 6000 BC the sea level was rising, transforming Britain into an island and cutting for ever the land bridge to the Continent over which the early migrants had passed with ease. Peat which covers so much of the uplands from a few inches to several feet thick had begun to form by 600 BC.

From about 8000–4000 BC, hunter-gatherer groups wandered on parts of Dartmoor. Stray artefact finds and scatters are, in the main, restricted to the lower slopes of the moor. Some woodland clearances from this period may be evidenced in the pollen record – though fires are not necessarily started by man!

From about 4000–2500 BC, Dartmoor was settled by early farming communities. These people left a few ritual monuments including chambered long barrows, cairns and dolmens, most of which are on the fringes of the moor. Subsequent prehistoric peoples, from 2500–1750 BC, left behind a variety of ritual and burial monuments: cairns, cists, stone rows, standing stones and stone circles. Sites of settlement are unknown.

During the period 1750–1000 BC, with the climate becoming much kinder than it is today, settlement became more widespread. The archaeological field evidence for this is spectacular – an array of irregular field systems, pounds, reaves, and hut circles, along with ritual monuments, For the next 500 years enclosed sites continued to be occupied, with new ones being established.

Towards the end of the first millenium BC a deterioration in the climate saw a decline in settlement on the high moor. However, there is evidence for the creation of new field systems at this time, with settlement activity, particularly on the edge of the moor.

The simplified chronological chart below is intended to provide an approximate dating for the various artefacts and sites recorded in this book.

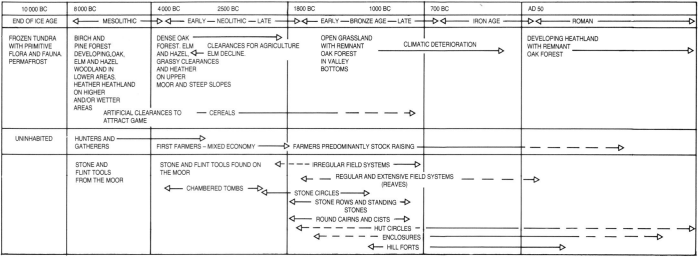

Based on information prepared by Dr. Alex Gibson (1988)

GREAT MIS TOR, MAIN CORE
(sx 562 770)

The central block, showing horizontal cracking with vertical faults beginning to appear.

GREAT MIS TOR

(sx 562 770)

Great Mis Tor is an avenue tor of several major blocks. From these, large
slabs have been split off by frost action to slide downwards and outwards
from the central mass.

GREAT MIS TOR
(sx 562 770)

With continued action by frost in the Ice Ages, the solid core of the tor
disintegrated. This mass of debris is known as 'clitter', and when taken for
use by man it is called moorstone.

PEAT

The granite base, with growan above, created an ideal surface for maintaining a waterlogged soil; perfect conditions for sphagnum moss to grow. Such conditions prevent decomposition of plant material, and layer upon layer of dead material builds up; this we call peat. Peat beds may be from a few inches to many feet thick.

MESOLITHIC MICROLITHS (*same size*)

These battered flakes collected by my brother, John Woods, from Soussons are carefully worked shapes and not chips. Flint does not occur naturally on Dartmoor, the nearest source being in East Devon.

BRONZE AGE BARBED AND TANGED ARROWHEAD (*same size*)

The mesolithic people produced a chisel-edged arrowhead (left), which evolved into a single-tanged arrowhead (page 39). The barbed and tanged arrowheads (above) are a later development (Hermon French Collection).

MESOLITHIC CHISEL ARROWHEAD  (*same size*)

NEOLITHIC STONE AXE (*same size*)

NEOLITHIC LEAF-SHAPED ARROWHEADS
(*same size*)

This Neolithic polished stone axe made of metamorphic rock was found at
Huccaby. The Neolithic people also had a distinctive leaf-shaped arrowhead
(Hermon French collection).

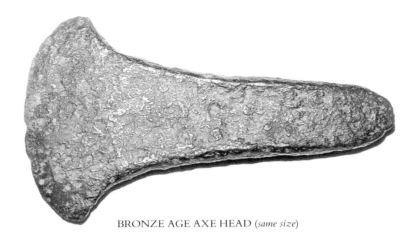

BRONZE AGE AXE HEAD (*same size*)

BRONZE AGE SINGLE-TANGED ARROWHEAD (*same size*)

This fine example of a Bronze Age axe-head was found on Corringdon Farm, South Brent. It is likely to date from the early Bronze Age. Though using metal, these migrants continued to rely on stone for many implements (Hermon French Collection).

SCRAPERS (*same size*)

SPINDLE WHORLS (*same size*)

Scrapers are difficult to date to a particular period.
This also applies to spindle whorls, for the Neolithic people began to
domesticate animals and the method of preparing thread was universal
down into historic times. The left hand example is made of clay the other
two of slate (Hermon French Collection).

# 2
# PREHISTORIC MEMORIALS, GRAVES AND RITUAL MONUMENTS

The simplest of all prehistoric memorials is the standing stone, or menhir. Few now remain standing, and it is likely that many were removed by later inhabitants.

The oldest manmade remains on Dartmoor are attributed to the Neolithic people who built stone tombs for their dead. These gallery or chambered tombs could not have contained all the dead of the community; elsewhere very large chambers held only a few dead, and some were re-used over a long period.

The variety of building and changes in design are numerous and may have been affected by the material available, or by the size of the community. On Dartmoor the much ravaged remains tend to be smaller compared to those found elsewhere in Britain and Europe. The larger design would be for three or four uprights, infilled with small stones, supporting a large capstone, the whole being covered by earth. The chamber was often offset to one end.

The well known Spinsters' Rock, known as a dolmen, illustrates the large uprights and capstone, but no trace of any mound remains. As there are similar constructions elsewhere without trace of covering material, the possibility exists that this dolmen was never actually covered.

Other burial sites of this period include: a long cairn, outside Stannon Newtake wall, near the stone row; a mound on the flank of Hameldown near Natsworthy; and below Haytor, two hundred yards from the Old Smith's Shop boundary rock is another possible site.

There are more than six hundred burial places of the Bronze Age on Dartmoor. Burial monuments include sites of individual interment in cists and pits below a variety of round cairn types, some no more than simple dumps of stone, with others being structured with kerbs, stone circles, or ring banks.

There appear to be no known Iron Age burials, though there were substantial numbers of early Iron Age people.

Some Bronze Age peoples buried their dead in a constricted position, in a simple chamber usually of five slabs, set level with the ground. The two shorter slabs were set inside the longer, covered by a single larger stone. The overall size varies, but this may only be due to the available material. The long side is usually orientated north-west/south-east. Once burial was completed, the cist was covered with a mound of earth and a retaining ring of stone set round the perimeter.

Construction and size varies. In some instances the stones lean outwards, and in others inward; in many cases the stones are packed together tightly and in others stand apart. One particular example sets the stones close together and by careful insertion they form a distinctive kerb. The majority have a single retaining wall but at least four have two rings, one has three, and three have four rings.

Cairns are mainly built of stone, barrows and tumuli are of earth construction. The majority of large cairns are predominant on the skyline and often grouped together. In many cases the cairn covers a small tor, as can be seen on Corndon and Rippon Tor.

Some cairns, such as those on Hameldown, have been dated to the rich Wessex Culture of 1550 B.C.

A further element in the building of cairns and cists is their frequent proximity to smaller rows of stone, of which at least seventy have been recorded. The purpose of these monuments is unknown. The majority of stones used are small when compared to the available stone close at hand. To add intrigue the stone nearest the grave is frequently much larger and in many cases reaches menhir proportions. The majority of rows are formed by a single line, many have two rows of roughly parallel lines and there are examples of five triple rows, plus several variants on the general theme.

Dartmoor's stone circles, twelve with diameters of over sixty feet, may be small in comparison to Stonehenge and Avebury, but they have an aura of their own. Much robbery has taken place and with the exception of Scorhill the stones are not very large. There is one example of twin circles, Grey Wethers, here the two circles come within six or seven yards of each other, and have been compared to the two inner rings of the great circle at Avebury.

On Shovel Down, Butterdon Hill, Merrivale, Fernworthy and Drizzlecombe there are so many monuments grouped together that they give the impression that here was a place of great ritual significance. None of these groups resembles another, and without positive dating, we cannot determine over what length of time these groups evolved.

The Shovel Down group is the most interesting, for it had at least eight stone rows, six of which are double; a possible stone circle; fourfold retaining rings; and the magnificent Longstone, terminal of a much robbed double row, which continues towards the Three Boys, a possible dolmen of which only one stone remains standing.

BEARDOWN MAN
(sx 596 797)

This magnificent stone stands a few yards from Devil's Tor and is not
very prominent unless approached from the north. Why these stones were raised
we do not know for they stand alone and are not apparently connected to any grave.

### LEE MOOR HANGING STONE
(sx 584 637)

The descriptive title 'Hanging stone' is self-explanatory. It has two interesting connections: first it stands in an ancient reave which we know dates from at least 1600 BC, and second it has engraved on one face the letters CB. These letters probably stand for Cholwich Bound, the only other case of a Cholwich Bound was recorded in the O.S. *Boundary Report Book* (1882–3) on a post near Tolchmoor Bridge, both are I fear lost in the upheaval of the China Clay works.

### WHIT MOOR STONE
(sx 633 896)

The Whit Moor menhir is surrounded by controversy simply because the knights who first perambulated the Forest in 1240 (in order to establish its boundary) did not mention its existence. Since then it has been used as a bound stone. The Duchy of Cornwall cut DC on its surface, South Tawton commoners cut TP and vulgarly infill their letters with paint, while for good measure the Throwleigh parishioners put T on two surfaces.

BUTTERDON DOWN
(sx 748 884)

MERRIVALE MENHIR
(sx 553 746)

LONGSTONE HILL
(sx 568 910)

BEACON PLAIN
(sx 657 593)

BEACON PLAIN
(sx 657 593)

HARBOURNE HEAD
(sx 696 651)

These are the remaining menhirs. Of the Butterdon Down stone little can be said, other than to say none of the major writers of the past mention it.

The Merrivale stone stands south of a number of other ritual monuments close to a stone circle, and on the ground a few yards away lies a stone which might also be a menhir. The triangular Harbourne Head stone has an early bench mark cut on one side. The two possible menhirs on Beacon Plain would have been the tallest on the moor when upright. Finally, the Longstone Hill stone is not I think granite but metamorphic rock.

CORRINGDON BALL – NEOLITHIC GRAVE
(sx 669 614)

The Neolithic grave near Corringdon Ball Gate is the best example out on the open moor. What is presumed to be the capstone, 11 feet long and up to 2 feet thick lies on the grass, close to four other large slabs, one of which may still be in its original upright position. The mound is visible, but the continuous close cropping by sheep of the grass which covers the whole area has meant it merges into the surrounding landscape. The mound is approximately 140 feet by 50 feet, with the chamber at the south end. It was built on the saddle between Corringdon Ball and Brent Fore Hill and is most conspicuous from the west when viewed from the multiple stone rows and retaining ring above the East Glaze Brook.

46

CORRINGDON BALL VIEWED FROM EAST GLAZE BROOK
(sx 669 614)

CUCKOO BALL NEOLITHIC GRAVE
(sx 659 583)

SPINSTERS' ROCK
(sx 703 908)

MEACOMBE NEOLITHIC GRAVE
(sx 725 879)

On the east slope of Cuckoo Ball the remains of another chambered tomb is distinguished by a group of seven stones, the two largest remain standing within an elongated mound.

Spinsters' Rock is similar to the quoits of Cornwall, it fell in 1862 and was incorrectly re-erected the same year. There is no trace of any mound.

In comparison the chambered tomb at Meacombe (on private land) is small, though its capstone gives it a substantial look. It is very difficult to distinguish a mound.

At the head of the River Sig, below the Ilsington–Bagtor Manor boundary rock, is a mound of earth and stone which may be a Neolithic grave. The bound has been called the Old Smith's shop, and charcoal has supposedly been found here, but there is no sign of any building. The mound on the other hand appears to consist of two parallel stone walls similar to the chambered cairn on Gidleigh Common. The question as to whether the Neolithic people on Dartmoor cremated their dead remains open. There are no capstones near the mound, but one of two hut circles close by does have very large door posts and it would be interesting to speculate that the destruction of Dartmoor remains began in the Bronze Age!

SIG HEAD NEOLITHIC GRAVE?
(sx 756 764)

RIPPON TOR CAIRN
(sx 747 756)

HOLNE MOOR CAIRNS
(sx 669 712)

There are three stone cairns on the peak of Rippon Tor one of which is built over the natural outcrop that forms the Tor. The hollow found in most cairns is due to past robbers or to over-energetic visitors. The cairn built close to the Drizzlecombe stone rows is known as the Giant's Basin.

DOWNTOR STONE ROW
(sx 587 693)

The Downtor stone row illustrates all the main features of a stone row. Small stones, increasing in size, form a single row with a stone of menhir proportions standing against the grave. This terminal stone was in recent times re-erected, and concreted into a hole of greater depth than the original builder scraped into the growan. The field evidence shows a much disturbed cist set within a retaining circle of moderately tall stones. The amount of earth would seem to indicate that the mound covering the cist was raised within the circle. At the far end, beyond the last stone, is another cairn.

YELLOWMEAD FOURFOLD RETAINING CIRCLES
(sx 575 678)

Near Yellowmead there is a fine example of a fourfold retaining circle.
When found it was mostly submerged in the soil and has since been brought
to the surface.

CIST ON LAKEHEAD HILL
(sx 645 776)

CROCK OF GOLD
(sx 615 731)

CIST, BLACK'S NEWTAKE
(sx 639 761)

CIST NEAR THE BLACKWATER
(sx 605 738)

The four examples of cists depicted above all have interesting features. The large cist on Lakehead Hill is an example of bad restoration. The capstone is an indication of its size, but it should have been re-erected with the chamber stones set down into the ground. Its accompanying row is not straight and enters the retaining circle. There are a number of cists close by with which it can be compared.

The chamber of the cist in Black's Newtake is an excellent example of the neatness and care taken in selecting stone for its construction.

The Crock of Gold cist, with its capstone thrown back, within a retaining circle, reflects in its name the hope of grave robbers. As these cists are all of the Bronze Age it is unlikely anything more than a few flints were ever found. These cists and that of the Blackwater are evidence that any suitable place could be chosen as the interment site, from the top of a hill, on its flank, or at the water's edge. There are several cists beside the Blackwater, close together to indicate a cemetery.

DRIZZLECOMBE MENHIR
(sx 592 670)

DRIZZLECOMBE MENHIR
(sx 592 670)

HURSTON RIDGE DOUBLE STONE ROW
(sx 674 825)

MERRIVALE DOUBLE STONE ROWS
(sx 555 748)

The Hurston Ridge stone row is one of the best on Dartmoor. Here we see a solid rectangular block set across the end of the row, while on the horizon next to the cist is another tall stone, of the other line, which on close inspection is triangular in shape. Compare the two menhirs of Drizzlecombe – one a very tall rectangular pillar the other a magnificent triangle.

Compare also the Lee Moor Hanging stone to that of the Harbourne Head triangle.

At Merrivale is another fine double row, which has a cairn in its centre from which another row projects at an angle, this row also has a twin running parallel to its course.

HEADLAND TRIPLE ROW
(sx 689 808)

The triple stone row on Headland Warren, one of five on the moor. Its far
end is cut by the tinners' excavations of Chaw Gully.

SCORHILL CIRCLE
(sx 655 874)

The Scorhill circle must have been very imposing when built, its tallest stone, eight feet high, still stands. Many of its stones would have stood five feet or more above the ground, and some of those taken from the circle have been used to strengthen the edge of the pot-water leat below the circle. Fortunately it has not been restored, unlike the twin circles of Grey Wethers. These two circles have been restored, but many visitors have noted the similarity and rectangular shape of their stones. Excavations here produced a quantity of charcoal.

GREY WETHERS TWIN CIRCLES
(sx 638 832)

RINGMOOR DOWN CIRCLE
(sx 565 655)

The Ringmoor Down circle demonstrates the simplicity of most Dartmoor circles, the stones are small in size and have an appeal all their own.

# 3
# PREHISTORIC HABITATION AND PASTORAL LIFE

The Mesolithic people were hunters and food gatherers who in the summertime wandered up on to the open highland, choosing to stay near a supply of fresh water. Apart from their microlith flints no other trace can be found of their passing.

The Neolithic people appear to have passed by in like manner, but in addition left us the remnants of their communal graves and scatters of artefacts possibly representing settlements. These were followed by the first Bronze Age inhabitants whose dwellings of wood and stone have been found in excavations by the Dartmoor Reaves Project on Holne Moor.

## Hut circles

The prehistoric builder of the familiar relic designated as 'hut circles' on maps, used many variations of four basic architectural styles. These were (1) A single wall of upright stones; (2) A double wall of upright stones with a rubble bank outside; (3) Rubble banks; (4) Coursed walling. There is no chronological determination possible from existing evidence.

The roof was made of strong boughs supporting a thatch, possibly of heather and turf, supported in some buildings by timber posts.

Hut circles vary in size from a rough diameter of nine feet to forty feet. They also vary considerably in shape for one can find near squares and rectangles, ovoids, semi-detached examples (two circles with a common wall), along with curious trefoil arrangements. The smallest may have been stores rather than dwellings, or for the lone herdsman tending his beasts. No one has ever counted the number of huts on the moor; Hansford Worth's estimate of two thousand may be more than 100 per cent out.

When the site was chosen, all the surface soil above the growan was scraped away and the internal wall built. The doorway, facing away from the prevailing wind, was narrow, between two and three feet wide. In some cases a 'porch' was built to give added protection. The entrance was paved, with one or two steps down, depending on the depth of soil removed.

Excavations have shown that some huts were partly paved, the amount of paving being very variable, perhaps the result of robbing? The hearth could be central, against the wall opposite the door, or to either side.

## Pounds

The word 'pound' on Dartmoor is descriptive of an enclosure. The enclosing pound wall comprised two drystone walls infilled with more rock, four to six feet, even up to nine feet wide, and up to six feet high. The areas enclosed are of infinite variety in shape and size, changes in direction being curved and not angled. Some walls are made with large slabs others with small blocks, depending upon the material available at each site.

Many sites enclose less than an acre, while the largest, Broadun, encloses fourteen acres, with over forty huts dotted randomly about. Other enclosures are devoid of stone huts, or contain from one upwards. These settlements may have been occupied for a considerable period, and as the community grew then an additional enclosure was added to the original. Ryders Rings is an excellent example. We also find pens for holding animals, built against the pound wall in many cases.

In addition to pounds there are clusters of huts forming larger settlements, such as those at Hartor and Swincombe, Standon Down, and at Watern Oke.

## Boundaries

Around 1750 BC it would seem various tribes or communities were in agreement on how to divide the land, and boundaries called reaves were constructed from stone and earth.

The rivers of southern Dartmoor run a long way into the moor, it could not, as seems to be the case, have been too difficult to agree a boundary line between the watersheds. For example the Eylesbarrow reave neatly divides the territory of the east bank of the River Meavy from that of the west bank of the River Plym, similarly the Three Barrows reave separates the valley lands of the rivers Erme and Avon.

On the rest of Dartmoor, community tracts have not followed quite such an identifiable pattern, and it appears that in some cases the rivers themselves have been used to designate a territorial boundary.

Once a community's land area was agreed with its neighbours, a reave was built to determine the boundary of land common to all. From this 'terminal reave' a close knit system of parallel walls subdivided the land into small plots or fields, dotted with homesteads.

When we look at farming communities we see up to four or five huts integral with a similar number of fields, such as is found on the west slope of White Ridge, or at Smallacombe Rocks near Haytor.

A charming individual settlement nestles between Saddletor and Rippon Tor, at Sig Head, where one hut in its own yard stands in a group of three fields. However, it must be remembered that the hut and fields may not be contemporary.

Larger farming communities are also found, twenty-seven huts being found within a complex of reaves which covers the area of Batworthy Corner to Teigncombe, and stretches south over Kestor, Middle Tor and Frenchbeer Tor.

We also find huts connected by droveways, and on Throwleigh Common four such huts form our first 'street'.

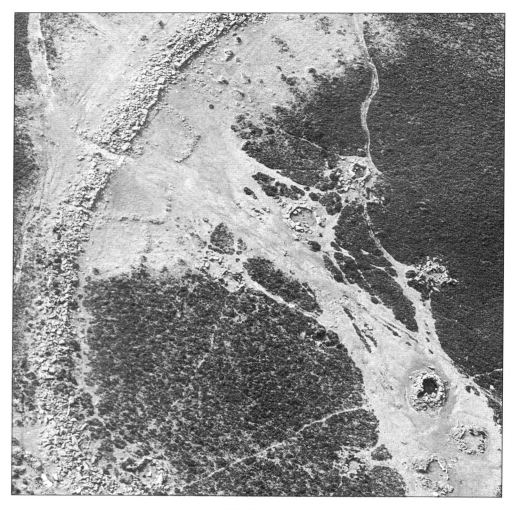

GRIMSPOUND
(sx 701 808)

This is the south-west segment of Grimspound. Thousands of visitors have
trampled a way through the wall at this point making an unnatural entrance
close to three animal pens built against the wall. The hut circle bottom right
has a secondary wall built out to protect the entrance from wind and rain.
Many features at Grimspound have been 'restored'.

ROUTRUNDLE
(sx 554 718)

There are two prehistoric pounds in this vicinity, surviving amidst medieval
fields whose walls are attached to the pounds. One shows no sign of
occupation, the other illustrated here, has one hut circle inside.

ENTRANCE TO GRIMSPOUND
(sx 701 808)

HUT CIRCLE, GRIMSPOUND
(sx 701 808)

HUT CIRCLE, BUSHDOWN
(sx 685 824)

The entrance used by the inhabitants of Grimspound is on the south, upper side, it is paved and its sides are made of massive slabs.

There are twenty-four huts inside the wall, the one depicted here can be seen bottom right of the aerial view at the head of this chapter, its entrance protected by a secondary wall.

This dwelling was carved into the valley side and has a magnificent view across the valley to the double stone row on Hurston Ridge and, prior to the Fernworthy plantations, extended views to Kestor.

HUT CIRCLE, EAST BOVEY HEAD
(SX 695 823)

There are several hut circles in the vicinity of East Bovey Head. Note the
very large slabs which form its inside wall and compare this to the hut on
Langstone Moor (p.64) which has a restored ring of medium size stones on
its interior, with earth and rubble on its exterior side.

HUT CIRCLE, LANGSTONE MOOR
(sx 557 778)

REAVE, GREAT VARRACOMBE
(sx 629 842)

REAVE, VENFORD TERMINAL
(sx 664 715)

GREAT WEST REAVE, WEST FLANK, ROOS TOR
(sx 543 766)

The common style of reave found on the moor today is in the form of a low mound running across the landscape, as seen in the Great Varracombe valley. In some instances reaves have been built upon to form the drystone walls of today. The Venford terminal reave is an excellent example of this, for as it rises from the west bank of the O Brook, the reave forms the base of the drystone wall as it runs over the ridge into the valley of the Swincombe. Parallel reaves can be seen abutting onto this terminal both here and on Holne Moor.

In Queen Elizabeth I's reign, a reave running up and through Three Barrows was described as 'a long conger of stones called Le Rowe Rew'.

This description is more suited to the Great West Reave as it descends from Roos Tor to Wedlake, for it meanders aimlessly down the hillside. Its make-up shows little use of earth, very much akin to the walls to be seen at Kestor.

WHITCHURCH COMMON PEDESTRIAN GATEWAY
(sx 530 750)

SIG HEAD HUT CIRCLE
(sx 753 757)

SHOVEL DOWN, ANIMAL GATEWAY
(sx 665 862)

To gain passage through the reave, openings were sometimes formed by placing large slabs at right angles either side of the gap. The two examples shown would seem to indicate the passage for humans and a large opening for stock. No evidence exists for us to determine the method of opening and closing the entrance.

SIG HEAD SETTLEMENT
(sx 753 757)

A charming individual settlement, nestles between Saddle Tor and Rippon Tor, at Sig Head, where one hut with a diameter of twenty-six feet stands in its own yard amidst three fields; the whole covers just over one acre. There appear to be two pens in the yard, and a small amount of soil build up against the lower walls indicates cultivation. The reave which runs down to the south-east corner should not be overlooked. The outline of the farm shows up fairly well in the evening light.

HORRIDGE COMMON HUT CIRCLES AND DROVEWAY
(sx 757 746)

Within the reave system small settlements of individual hut circles are quite common. In the case of Horridge Common two huts of such a settlement are joined by a short droveway. Droveways provided access through the parallel reave system, and this is clearly seen at Kestor. An interesting feature is the hut circle within a ring that can be seen at Foales Arrishes, a late Bronze/Iron Age settlement. Another example is the Round Pound on Chagford Common.

FOALES ARRISHES
(sx 738 758)

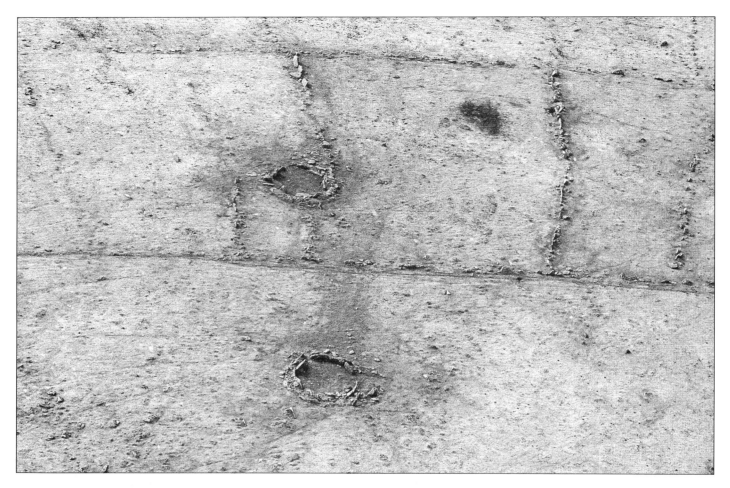

KESTOR SETTLEMENT, TEIGNCOMBE COMMON
(sx 666 869)

This aerial photograph shows a very small part of this absorbing settlement. It reveals one wall, to the right (west) of the hut circle with its own field or pen. This was not included in Dr Curwen's drawings of the site, used by Lady Fox in her excavations. Many aerial photographs cover such large areas that much interest is lost. In this case the Round Pound has been excluded from view, enabling the reader to distinguish sufficient detail to relate this to the photographs taken on the ground.

PAVED ENTRANCE TO ROUND POUND HUT CIRCLE
(sx 664 868)

Excavation of this hut circle by Lady Fox showed it to be both the home and workshop of an Iron Age blacksmith. Within the hut were found a furnace, quenching-pit and anvil, the hut being one of the largest on the moor.

HUT CIRCLES, KESTOR SETTLEMENT
(sx 666 869)

These hut circles can be distinguished in the preceding aerial photograph. Note the large block interior wall and the earth and rubble on the outside.

KESTOR SETTLEMENT FIELD WALL
(sx 666 869)

This wall, in excellent preservation, would not hold animals unless reinforced with thorns.

DROVEWAY
(sx 664 868)

This is the lower or northern droveway of the two that bisect the Kestor
Settlement. This portion leads to the Round Pound and both sides show a
lack of earth in their construction.

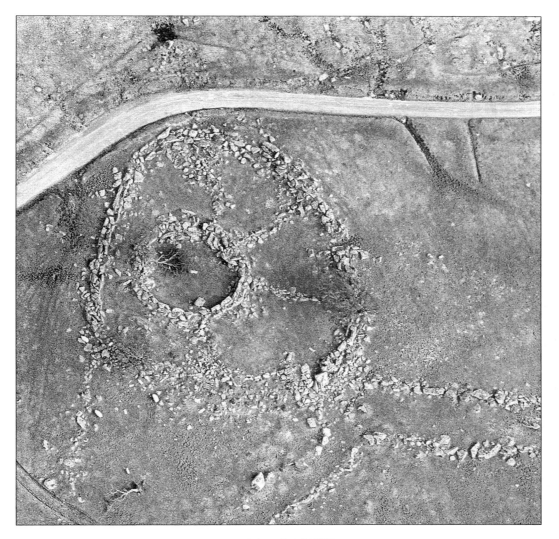

THE ROUND POUND
(sx 664 868)

The pound was used in medieval times and it may be that at that time the
spokes (walls) which divide the pound were built. Note how the droveway
detours to the pound before continuing on across the common.

# 4
# INSCRIBED STONES
# OF THE
# POST-ROMAN PERIOD

The post-Roman period covers the fifth to the seventh centuries AD, and it is from this time that the stones, described in this chapter, date.

The Roman occupation of Britain from AD 43 lasted approximately four hundred years. Soon after the Roman evacuation Germanic tribes arrived: Saxons, Angles and Jutes.

The West Saxons were in some measure of control by AD 670, and the Kingdom of British Dumnonia was well established. It was a period of considerable turmoil but the Saxons held out against invaders until 1066, except for a short period when Cnut and his son Hardicnute held majesterial power. It was in this twilight period that Christianity came to Britain.

Finds of imported Mediterranean ware at Lydford, and the dedication of some churches to celtic saints, are regarded as evidence of the occupation of at least the lower slopes of Dartmoor during this period.

It is against this background we can consider the inscribed stones of this period. The present writer researched these many years ago when there were five such stones, a sixth had been removed to the British Museum. Since then two other stones have come to light; one has been set up on the green at Sourton, the other is on private land near Bagtor. This latter stone, if it is of this period, would appear to be the oldest for it is decorated with what is purported to be Ogam script. Tom Greeves, who brought it to light, is by no means certain that this is correct.

The readers' attention is here drawn to the other inscribed stones of the period, three of which are in the vicarage garden at Tavistock, where the nineteenth century antiquarian, Reverend Bray, gathered them together.

A memorial stone was recently re-erected at Sourton Cross, and another is to be seen in Lustleigh Church.

INSCRIBED STONES OF THE POST-ROMAN PERIOD          △ = Inscribed stone

SABINI FILI MACCODECHETI
(SX 482 743)

Translates as 'The Stone of Sabinus, the Son of Maccodechet'. The letter forms are a mixture of normal, late-Roman capitals (the S, B and D), devolved or later developed capitals (the A with the bent cross bar), and lower case, or cursive forms (like the h) which had begun to creep into monumental inscriptions from manuscript writing. These forms were later copied on all kinds of inscriptions. It is the combination of these various forms which give the best dating indications, about AD 550; or before St Augustine's crusade of AD 597.

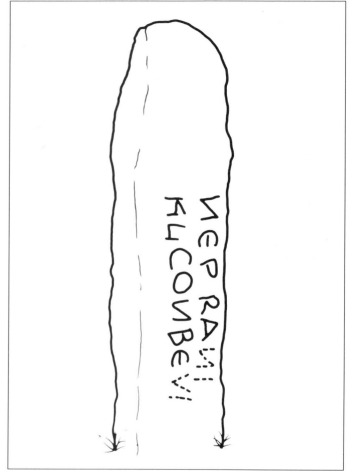

NEPRANI FILI CONBEVI
(sx 482 743)

This is a very large stone standing a good seven feet tall, approximately two feet across the front, with a depth of ten inches. Unfortunately in its present position, the front with its engraved inscription faces into a hedge. The inscription translates as 'The Stone of Nepranus, the Son of Conbevus'; the letter forms are fairly devolved and the stone can reasonably be dated around AD 550.

DOBVNNI FABRI FILI ENABARRI
(sx 482 743)

This third stone in the vicarage garden is the smallest, standing only five feet tall; fifteen inches across the front and with a depth of twelve inches. It originally stood beside a track across Roborough Down in the parish of Buckland Monachorum. It had been used as a gatepost and the iron hinges are still embedded in one side. The stone itself has been carefully trimmed to shape. The words on its face are engraved on the top half of the stone whereas other stones are inscribed on the middle third, which might suggest it was lopped off at a convenient height to form the gatepost.

It has sustained considerable damage and wear, and is overgrown with lichen making it very difficult to decipher the words.

Susan Pearce, Curator of Antiquities of Exeter Museums, provided the author with the following information: 'This stone is a well known problem piece. Macalister read it as DOBVNNI FABRI FILI ENABARRI. The gist of the translation is "The Stone of Dobonnus the Son of Enabarr". The Fabri has sometimes been interpreted as meaning Smith.'

What also makes this stone fascinating is its Ogam inscription, primitive runic or Irish script based on the Latin alphabet. It is interpreted by groups of straight lines either side of a vertical plane, horizontal or obliquely, in sets of 1 to 5 lines. Each letter is achieved in its simplest form. For example 'a' is represented by a single horizontal line on both sides of the plane, 's' by four horizontal lines to the right of the plane and 'r' by five oblique lines on either side of the plane.

On this stone the vertical plane is the left hand front edge of the block with those letters extended on either side being set at right angles. Ogam is read from the bottom up and as this stone is very worn at the edges it is almost indecipherable, though it is certainly there and probably reads 'Enabarr'. Again this stone can be dated around AD 550 or a little earlier. The Sabini and Enabarr stones and the single Ogam inscription are important evidence of Irish influence.

77

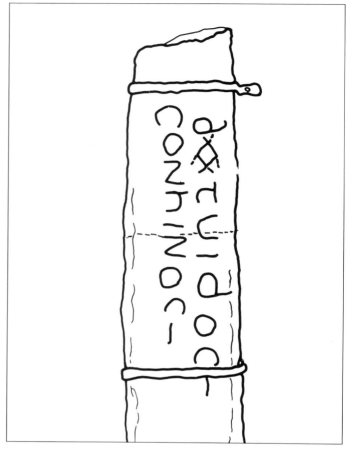

DATUIDOCI CONHINOCI FILIUS
(sx 785 813)

If the Enabarr stone is a problem piece, the Lustleigh Stone appears to be equally enigmatic. In its previous position it was set in the floor at the threshold of the church and its surface has been worn smooth by the feet of people entering the church over many centuries. Parts of the church date from the twelfth century and the list of rectors dates back to 1262. The stone has now been moved and stands clamped to the wall of the nave, near the Norman font. It has been cracked across its middle.

Susan Pearce states that the usually accepted reading of this stone is

DATUIDOCI CONHINOCI FILIUS translated as 'The Stone of Datuidoc, the Son of Conhinoc' and judging by the letter forms might be dated about AD 580–600 or even a little later. 'Filius' is indecipherable, though Macalister claims to have seen it.

The graveyard has all the features of an early Christian burial ground, facing east-west, with the earth piled high, surrounded by a trench which is now the roadway.

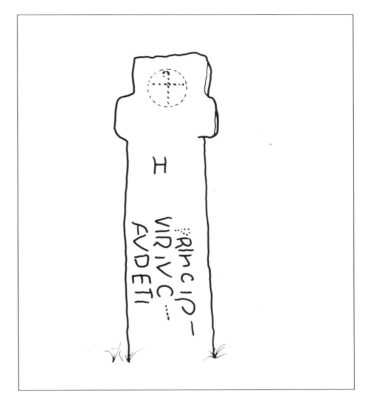

PRINCIPI VIRIVCI AUDETI
(sx 547 918)

This stone has unfortunately been known to have stood in other places, it is hoped soon to be in its rightful place, or at least very near to its original position. However, its removal during the construction of the Okehampton bypass has left some doubt as to its final resting place. In its time it has also been re-used as a direction stone, for on each face are engraved the letters H for Hatherleigh, T for Tavistock, O for Okehampton, and L for Launceston; this was done in the eighteenth century.

Masson Phillips suggests the stone has been re-cut to form a cross, and this may be so, as a cross head would have been unusual on an early Christian memorial. If originally a cross, then it would be the oldest on Dartmoor.

The stone appears to have been erected on a Roman road that skirted the north side of Dartmoor, running from Exeter into Cornwall. Its most important feature is one of the three words which run vertically on the shaft of the cross. The word PRINCIPI is clearly decipherable, whereas the other two VIRIVCI AUDETI are not, but are reasonable interpretations of the engravings.

The term 'principi' denotes a 'chief' or 'leader' and was used as a title in the late Roman Empire. Following the general theme of inscriptions on early Christian memorials the other words would have been the name of the man commemorated.

Above the engraved H on the front face there is a very faint design which some say is a very devolved Chi-rho form, the first letters of Christ's name in Greek, again an early Christian decoration.

Because the stone has been moved, re-used and is very worn, it cannot be dated with accuracy but its letter forms suggest about AD 550.

SAXON MEMORIAL, SOURTON GREEN
(sx 535 904)

This stone, standing beside the Okehampton–Tavistock Road, is of Saxon origin of the tenth century. Until recently the stone was in two pieces, and was used to prop up the roof of a nearby farm building. With much local help the stone was repaired and re-erected on the village green by the National Park Authority, in 1986.

# 5

# BOUNDARIES, FOREST AND PASTURE

The Saxon advance into Devon appears to have been complete by the beginning of the eighth century AD. Despite the dominance of Anglo-Saxon placenames in the County, the paucity of culturally distinct artefacts and monuments from the period 8th–11th centuries, indicates a relatively small colonization on Dartmoor.

An example of a strip field lies on the east side of the road from Widecombe to the Dunstone turn-off, this being part of the ancient manor of Dunstone recorded in the Domesday Book and might have been the original manor lands. The whole of this area of fields lies on top of the massive Rippon Tor reave system and reveals a startling similarity between the parallel reave complex and Saxon strip fields.

## Boundaries

Having occupied the land it became necessary to define the boundary of occupation. It is not possible to say who first raised a bound stone on Dartmoor, but on crossing the north-west flank of Shovel Down early one morning and overlooking a prehistoric settlement whose reaves criss-crossed the landscape, the author was struck by the taller stone set at junction points.

The Saxons and those that followed carefully delineated their land boundaries. The Saxons settled the land under a 'Lord of the Manor', whose lands were later overlaid by the parish, which may, like Buckland-in-the-Moor contain but one manor, or a number, for example, Widecombe which is subdivided by six manors.

The first choice as a marker was a prominent natural feature, which could be qualified under the description that it had been there 'tyme out of mind'. We therefore find tors, rivers, cairns, standing stones etc., used to establish boundaries. Widecombe Parish uses rivers for many miles of its boundary.

In much later years, names and initials, even dates, were engraved on natural rocks or on set stones, marked as 'BS' or 'B Rock' on the Ordnance Survey maps.

A century ago, 1882–3, the Ordnance Survey carried out work to establish the correct parish boundaries. The surveyor produced a *Boundary Report Book* in which was recorded the boundary, plus any inaccuracies, and agreed remedy. The surveyor was accompanied by meresmen – mere being an old word for boundary – people who knew the boundary.

Sergeant J. J. Ford perambulated the boundary of the Forest of Dartmoor and the parishes that ajoin it, this being twenty-two of the some forty parishes which can be found in the Dartmoor area. He was careful to ensure that his meresmen knew the boundary and whenever necessary he would include an enlarged sketch or written description. An extract from a Report Book reveals:

*William Hutchings (Moorman) employed as Meresman for Lydford, was acquainted with a portion of the boundary of Dartmoor with which the Meresmen appointed by the Clerk of the Peace were not. Lt. Col. R.D. Jones consent obtained previous to employing him.*

*James Rouse (Overseer of the Parish of Gidleigh) acted as Meresman for that parish, in consequence of the illness of the Meresman appointed by the Clerk of the Peace who were unable to attend.*

*John Perryman (Miller & Farmer) acted as Meresman for Chagford owing to the illness of one of the meresmen appointed by the Clerk of the Peace; the other appointed Meresman was not acquainted with the side of the Parish perambulated.*

*John Edmunds (Moorman) employed as meresman for Ugborough, he being well acquainted with the boundary of the Moors and renting the South quarter of Dartmoor.*

James J. Ford

SERGT, R.E. 8/6/82.

When the agreed boundary was recorded, the meresmen signed the book, in the case of William Hutchings he made his mark instead.

In 1204 King John disafforested Devon except Exmoor and part of Dartmoor. He should then, under Forest laws, have set the bounds of the Forest; whether this was done or not we do not know. King John has always been depicted as a man who put self-interest first.

King Henry III in granting the Forest of Dartmoor to his brother Richard, Earl of Cornwall, probably had a shrewd idea what the grant entailed, and the Knights who surveyed and set out the bounds of the first recorded perambulation in 1240 also had a sound basis on which to work. These knights made a straightforward survey: they named boundary points and took a direct line between each, except where they followed the course of a river. The names they used are not now easily identifiable with a bound, and discrepancies in the perambulation are frequent. Another major perambulation occurred in 1608 and the lack of certainty is evident:

*FFIRST they p'sent that the bounds of the fforest of Dartmoore as they the said jurors do fynde partlie by coppies of auncient recordes ptlie. upon the evidence of other p'sons and ptlie. upon their owne knowledge, but especiallie as the boundes have been and are used and accustomed to be . . .*

Such uncertainties do allow freedom to consider one's own interpretation. For instance the present Forest boundary goes by way of Watern Tor and Manga Rock to the Langstone. In 1240 it descended to 'Watesbrokelakesfote' (the confluence of the Wallabrook and Teign) and thence to the Langestone by way of the Heigheston. This latter bound does not seem to exist today, but the 'highest stone' is the tallest of the two menhirs, now fallen, which abut the fourfold circle. When standing they would have formed a reasonably straight line over Shovel Down. This stone is in fact marked with GP, Gidleigh Parish, and if raised may reveal on another face the letter C for Chagford. Knowing the moorman and parishioners of the commons, they would have no difficulty in taking a nibble out of the King's lands, which in effect the current boundary seems to indicate.

Many of the parishes marked their bounds, sometimes with their full name, sometimes with just an initial and sometimes with an additional letter, B for Bound, or P for Parish. Interpretation is not always straightforward because the brevity of the lettering can cause confusion. The letters WB can stand for Walkhampton Bound, or Whitchurch Bound – both parish bounds – Willsworthy Bound, a manor, or Warren Bound. Sampford Spiney adds the letter P, usually below the SS. The single letter B can stand for Bovey (North Bovey Parish), Buckland which is both a parish and a manor, Bagtor which is a manor in Ilsington Parish, or Bedford (The Duke of Bedford).

Some boundstones have been given the additional distinction of a date, presumably when they were erected. On the Ashburton boundary, close to the site of New House, an extinct carter's stop on the track from Ashburton to Chagford, there is a natural earthfast boulder engraved A1793. Halsanger Manor bound is engraved PW 1746 (there are two of these on the manor boundary), and a study of the *Boundary Report Books* reveals that on the Okehampton/Sampford Courtenay boundary there is a stone inscribed OP/B1697, SP/B1697, the earliest dated boundstone known.

Exactly when Dartmoor first became a Forest is not known, Rowe suggests it may date from Cnut's *Constitutiones de Foresta* and quotes Manwood's *Treatise of the Laws of the Forest*, written in 1615 for the definition that 'A Forest is a certain territorie of woody grounds and fruitful pastures, privileged for wild beasts and fowles of the Forest, chase and warren, to rest and abide in the safe protection of the king, for his princely delights and pleasure.' The Forest was therefore very important to the king and was a mainstay of his larder.

A document issued in the later years of Henry VIII's reign lays down the rights of commoners within the King's Forest. For instance they could pasture as many 'Catell as they maye wynter upon these holdyngs come to the Kyngs Forrest by Sonne and goo home by Sonne'. This was an excellent measure for controlling the number of animals and ensuring that the owner would only pasture those he could maintain in winter on his own lands. No doubt the farmer abused these numbers whenever he got the chance, and to get round the decree that he could only take his beasts onto the Forest between sunrise and sunset, he built a fold close to the edge of the Forest for securing his animals at night. The commoner might also have 'all that maye doo hym good excepte grene ocke and venyson'.

## Cornditches, pounds and gateposts

The commoners also had to build 'Cornedychis' to keep the deer in the Forest, this was the physical barrier made by digging a deep ditch and throwing the earth behind a stone facia. Deer, who are natural jumpers, could not see over the wall and were deterred from leaping over, but once over the way back was quite easy and that suited the King very well. Later a wall was built above the mound.

To give access through the cornditch 'leapyeats' were built, and it was commanded that these gates must be kept in good repair. There are many records of court action against those who were derelict in their duty.

Dartmoor farmers developed a unique system of gateposts prior to the nineteenth century, based on a variety of grooves

into which bars of varying length were inserted. Many of these slotted posts are still in situ, though they were sometimes turned round when iron hinges became fashionable.

The Forest was divided into quarters, each with its own pound. The oldest on record is Dunnabridge Pound, mentioned in a document of 1342. The others are Erme Pound, Halstock and Creber, the latter being an area of open land surrounded by fields through which two 'strolls' have been left for access.

Outside the walls of Erme Pound are two shelters, one which has a stone bench for people to sit on. Just inside the gate of Dunnabridge Pound is a keeper's shelter. Records also show that there were stocks for offenders here as well. An example of public stocks can be seen at Belstone. Regular drifts were held, it being customary to drive ponies on one day and horned cattle on another, strays being impounded in the appropriate pound until the fine was paid. Individual manors also had pounds for holding strays.

## Cultivation

The Saxon farmer would clear the land to the best of his ability before cultivation. Those rocks he was able to move formed the walls of his fields, while the larger earthfast boulders had to remain where they were. It is only in recent years, with the aid of grants and the mechanical digger, that further clearance been made so that modern deep ploughs could be used. Now small man-made tors appear in the corner of fields.

Following removal of the stone, land was pared of its surface vegetation, which was burnt and then ploughed in. The plough was drawn by oxen and a 'two-bill' used to dig round any obstruction. The iron head of this instrument had a narrow digger on one side and a chopper on the other for cutting roots. A man-powered breast-plough was later also used.

Land was either worked in severalty – with individual, often irregular, fields designated as a single holding – or communally. The practice of dividing arable land into strips is associated with nucleated settlement and shows itself either as strip lynchets or, less commonly, as ridge and furrows.

There are many references to oxen in the records but visual evidence can be seen if we study the lynchets on the western flank of the Challacombe valley which are plainly visible in the evening light. Each strip is approximately one furlong in length (one furrow long), though many are of greater length. The bank ends dovetail into one another, the explanation being that to plough with oxen, that are unwieldy to turn, a space had to be left at the end of each strip for this purpose.

At the head of this valley another method of cultivation can be seen. These are 'lazybeds', where ridges two feet to eight feet wide were formed by hand-digging and throwing the soil from a ditch up to a yard wide between the beds to give a greater depth of soil.

Also practised was the system of infield/outfield agriculture. The infields, closest to the farms, were under more or less permanent cultivation. Beyond lay the outfields, occasionally cultivated, but usually under pasture.

## Walls and hedgerows

Perhaps the most evident use of stone on Dartmoor is in its use by man to build walls. Of great variety, from the roughly constructed drystone bank, to the most solid of quarried-stone barriers, granite walls snake their way across miles of moorland like craggy serpents.

As the land was cleared of naturally occurring and abundant moorstone, so it was used in the building of field boundaries and enclosures, each taking on individual characteristics from the size and shape of the stones in the immediate area. Where a large, immovable rock stood, it was simply incorporated into the wall. Any convenient stone was utilised, and no doubt many archaeological features have been lost to energetic wall-builders in the past. Detours were negotiated around boggy land, resulting in sudden deviations in line.

The builders showed great skill in producing a 'smooth' and a 'rough' face on many walls, the smooth side facing onto the common, thus deterring others' stock from entering. In some cases, to make the wall more stable, it was capped with flat stones.

Older walls generally comprise small stones, roughly built up, and one can, as the moormen say, 'see daylight through them'. In some later walls, cut stone is used, and the marks of feather and tare are often visible. Sledges dragged by ponies would have been used to transport large blocks. These would then have been lifted using a tripod arrangement, or ramps, and levered into place with considerable human effort.

Some walls were built with two stone faces, infilled with earth and rubble. Such stone-faced hedgebanks may be considerably older than drystone walls, and are a particularly prominent feature of the 'in country' surrounding the upland moor. Some have been planted with beech trees to act as shelterbelts.

The advent of barbed wire, the introduction of adventurous and athletic Scottish blackface sheep, and the loss of cheap labour, has led to the decline of wall-building generally. Many old walls are in a poor state of repair due to damage by stock, or merely by weathering. The Dartmoor National Park Authority now assists with repairs, either financially, or advisory, where there is public benefit.

## Sheep

The largest medieval agricultural industry on the moor was the keeping of sheep. It is said that at one time 120 000 sheep grazed over the commons and Forest, and this in turn fuelled a flourishing woollen industry.

Such were the shepherd's responsibilities he was the only person excused from going to church. In some parts of the country when a shepherd died, he would be buried with a wisp of wool in his hand, so that St Peter would know to let him pass through the golden gates into Heaven.

## Warrens

Another important agricultural pursuit in medieval times was the rearing of rabbits for food and for their skins. Some four thousand rabbits were on the menu at the enthronement of the Archbishop of York in 1485.

The rabbit, like the Dartmoor pony, is not indigenous to these islands and is thought to have been introduced as a source of food by the Normans. The word rabbit originally referred to the young animal, full grown it was known as a coney, derived from the Latin *cuniculus* – a burrowing animal.

Risdon gives the earliest known reference to warrening: 'Trowlesworthy Warren, in the Parish of Shaugh, was granted before the date of deeds, by Baldwin de Redvers, Earl of Devon, to Sampson de Tralesworthy, at some period between the years 1135 and 1273.'

The evidence of this industry on Dartmoor remains in abundance. In broad terms a warren consists of an area of land bounded by natural features or markers, a warren house and out-buildings, and a specially constructed habitat for rabbits. Peaty soil is not conducive to natural rearing so the warrener provided the best artificial aids he could, and this meant he built a 'bury' (sometimes called 'pillow mounds') for his charges.

The various methods of warrening on Dartmoor are well documented elsewhere, although the author has gained further information recalling how rabbits were farmed, in particular at the Headland Warren.

This warren, and associated fields, known as the 'Four Aces', can clearly be seen from the Princetown to Moretonhampstead road as it passes the Warren House Inn. In the years during the First World War, it is said, rabbits were kept inside these gateless 'fields' which were thickly planted with gorse. This information was given to the author by Bob Haynes, who was informed by an old man, Peter Hannaford of Sherrill, who worked for the warrener, John Hannaford.

Somewhat at variance with this information is the story related by Freda Wilkinson. She tells of how her friend, Leonora Bray, helped to catch rabbits at Headland Warren during the 1920s. The warrener left open a creep hole in the wall of the 'field', one containing sweet grass to tempt the rabbits to enter. He then netted the hole while Leonora, with the aid of a lantern scared the rabbits, making them bolt back through the opening and into the net. Freda Wilkinson also reported that the warrener grew turnips (swedes) in the playing card plats (the 'Aces'), to feed the rabbits in winter.

This conflicting information may simply mean that both methods of warrening were used, although there is little outward sign that the fields in question were ever cultivated. Viewing the hillside from a distance reveals no apparent change in vegetation inside or outside the rabbit-proof walls. Yet looking back at the small plot used by the miners just to the north east of the Warren House, we see a green oasis amidst the heather, a sure sign of recent cultivation. Why then no grass or gorse in the 'Four Aces'?

Mrs Hannaford speaking to the author's mother, said that in 1915 they did not cultivate the fields because of the 'gokos' (phonetic spelling of a word she'd not heard before), the bluebells, which in season still turn the Challacombe Valley blue. Simon Butler confirms that a folk-name for bluebells is 'cuckoos', ('guckoos' in Devon).

This pretty menace has not intruded into the western 'fields', neither has bracken – which soon takes over vacated cultivated land – though it is found in abundance in the Vitifer mine complex below the 'Four Aces'. However, a closer look at the field directly west of the Warren House, over the ridge in the Redwater Valley, reveals that it is covered with bracken, and that earth has slipped to rise level with the top of the lower wall, clear evidence that this 'Ace' was cultivated. This indicates that both methods of warrening, described above, were in use in the early decades of this century.

TEIGNHEAD FARM GATEWAY
(sx 635 844)

This gateway is one of a variety based on individual bars fitting into slots of various shapes, in this case the slot in the left-hand post is of the L-shaped type. Teignhead farm was built about 1790 so that this form of gatepost was being used then. When they originated is not known but Ordolf sometimes thought to be 'Childe the Hunter' was known for his athleticism and was said to be 'capable of breaking the strongest gate bars'.

THE EARLIEST BOUNDSTONE?
(sx 654 865)

The prehistoric settlement on the north-west flank of Shovel Down. Here it is noticeable that at the junction of boundary walls a taller stone is emplaced.

WARREN BOUND
(sx 640 924)

The people of South Zeal and the Duchy of Cornwall agreed the boundary of Skaigh Warren in the nineteenth century. There are two bound stones engraved SZ1/DC1 and SZ2/DC2 marking the extent of the warren.

## A SELECTION OF FOREST BOUNDS

HEIGHESTON
(sx 659 860)

Over many centuries the bounds of the Royal Forest of Dartmoor have been disputed, changed and marked in various ways. It is the author's unsubstantiated theory that the fallen menhir abutting the fourfold retaining circle near Batworthy Corner is the 'Heigheston' of the 1240 perambulation. It lies directly as stated between the confluence of the Wallabrook and Teign ('Wotesbrokelakesfote') and the Longstone ('Langestone').

This tall stone is engraved with the letters GP for Gidleigh Parish, and possibly C for Chagford on the other. The 1608 perambulation for some reason has two bounds: Arme Headd, the old spelling of the River Erme,

and Broad Rock only two hundred yards apart with a definite kink in the line. The A Head stone is about central to the course of the river below, but it is possible that in the passing centuries the Erme has cut its way further north. Broad Rock has on its surface the letters BB for the manor of Blatchford. Burt, in the preface to Carrington's poem Dartmoor says the letters BB/LB should be on its surface, LB for Lydford Bound.

The *Boundary Report Books* show three 'iron bar' bounds, but a stone at Eylesbarrow which now has an iron bar, flattened at the top with the letters FB, Forest Bound, WB, Walkhampton Bound, would mean a fourth.

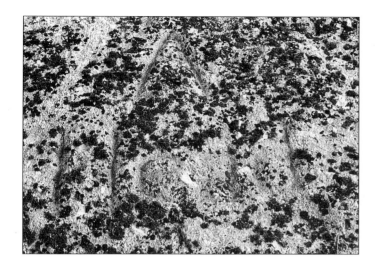

A HEAD
(sx 620 673)

BROAD ROCK
(sx 618 673)

EYLESBARROW
(sx 599 687)

PARISH BOUNDS

SAMPFORD SPINEY
(sx 533 735)

Parish bounds come in all shapes and sizes, both on set stones and rocks. The Sampford Spiney bounds are all clearly marked, this one positioned to show that the main core of Pu Tor is not in that parish. It is noticeable that landmarks such as tors are fixed in one parish or manor and are not astride the boundary.

WALKHAMPTON/LIDFORD
(sx 575 750)

Near Princetown, opposite to where the Rundlestone once stood is a bound, a cut stone with WALK/HAMP/TON on one face and LID/FORD on the other. Seldom does the light seem right to make the deciphering of these letters easy. This stone was recorded in the *Boundary Report Book* as being out of position. It has not been replaced, but the correct line a few yards further west is now marked by a line of granite posts. It is possible that someone tried to get the line set so that the row of now ruined dwellings to the north were outside the Forest, with consequently no dues payable to the Duchy of Cornwall.

OKEHAMPTON/SAMPFORD COURTENAY
(sx 607 967)

Several bounds are dated, the oldest is off the moor between Okehampton and Sampford Courtenay, engraved OP/B 1697, SP/B 1697.

On the Ashburton boundary is a rock with A1793, and between Lee Moor and Shaugh Moor is a stone marked LM 1835 and SM 1835. A deviation from this is a line of stones marking the Ashburton/Buckland boundary, which in addition to the A and B cut on their surfaces, have the letters EPB 1837. In the previous year, 1836, the Bastard family woke up one morning to find tinners cutting a leat across the front of their house. The tinners felt by ancient custom they could do this without regard to others' property, but they eventually lost the ensuing court case. It is probable that Edward Pollexfen Bastard had his initials and date engraved on these stones thereby stating, 'this is my land, keep out'.

ASHBURTON
(sx 742 757)

LEE MOOR/SHAUGH MOOR
(sx 568 634)

BUCKLAND/ASHBURTON
(sx 740 743)

## MANOR BOUNDS

PW 1746
(sx 739 754)

BAGTOR MANOR
(sx 756 764)

What has been said about other bound stones is of course true of manor bounds.

The Woodley family held Halsanger Manor for several centuries until 1925, and there are two stones engraved PW 1746 (Philip Woodley) on their boundary. Again not just set stones are used but also prominent rocks, as can be seen on the Ilsington/Bagtor line. This bound is also known as the Blacksmith's Shop.

In the years 1853/4 the Duke of Somerset had the bounds of his land defined with set stones bearing the letters DS and the date, either 1853 or 1854. This was probably done to clearly define his property, because he was then in his late 70s. The highest in the land were known by their initial, S for Somerset, B for Bedford, etc. The work was carried out by the local steward. On the reverse side of these stones are individual names for each boundary point, some being very old. Others, such as those running over Haytor Down, are new, and here can be found Prince of Wales, Victoria, Old Jack and Prince Albert. But there is always some intriguing point arising. For instance on this line is Wm/STONE, known as William Stone. On its reverse is the date 1853, no DS (note the old bench mark), and the stone is a crude block, not like the champfered stones which must have been additional markers to the older bound to which Wm belongs. The first stone of this line is a moorstone slab with the letters PB, Parish Bound.

1853 (Wm STONE)
(sx 771 779)

VICTORIA (DS 1853)
(sx 766 783)

POUND, SOUTH HARTON
(sx 768 822)

The term pound denotes an enclosure whether prehistoric, Forest quarter or manor, or those built on the moor by the moorman to hold his charges, sheep, cattle or ponies. One such can be seen outside Stannon Newtake on White Ridge, and appears to have the ruins of a building on its south side. Both Erme and Dunnabridge Pound had shelters for the keeper; there were also stocks at Dunnabridge. Another fine set of stocks remain at Belstone.

RUINS OF BUILDING ERME POUND
(sx 637 657)

POUND, WHITE RIDGE
(sx 648 816)

BELSTONE STOCKS
(sx 619 935)

LYNCHETS
(sx 694 799)

The lynchets, so clearly seen in the evening light on Challacombe Down, are
the result of strip ploughing, here by oxen. The method was to clear the land
of rocks, piled as a wall. The subsequent cultivation on a steep slope caused
the earth to slip either by the act of ploughing or by climatic conditions,
eventually the earth reached the top of the wall forming the effect known as
a lynchet.

LAZYBEDS
(sx 694 824)

Another method of cultivation is the 'lazybed' where earth is thrown up to form a pile, so that the depth of soil is doubled, leaving a ditch between the beds. This can be seen on the west bank at East Bovey Head, just beyond the head of the West Webburn of the Challacombe valley.

## STONE WALLS

NEWTAKE WALL
(sx 664 752)

Where enclosures meet the moor, many walls show distinctive 'rough' and
'smooth' faces. The smooth side faced on to the common to prevent stock
entering the enclosures.

NEWTAKE WALL

Large immovable stones are simply incorporated into the general construction.

NEWTAKE WALL, NEAR TWO BRIDGES
(sx 623 747)

During the nineteenth century many walls were built using roughly squared blocks of stone. One of the first to introduce this style was John Bishop of Swincombe, whose work, in his own words, was 'ordained to stand'. He was once asked how he managed to get such large stone into position. He replied 'Aw, tis surprisin' what 'e can do with a laiver (lever) or two.'!

DOUBLE-SKINNED WALL, DUNNABRIDGE
(sx 645 746)

Stone walls are a vital component of the Dartmoor landscape and their conservation is an unending task. Here, through a government sponsored project, the Duchy of Cornwall, with the co-operation of the tenant, has reinstated a considerable length of walling. Such projects bring landscape and farming benefits; they help with the maintenance of traditional rural skills and in some cases create local employment.

## GATEPOSTS

WOODENSTONE GATE HANGER, COCKS TOR
(sx 522 762)

WOODENSTONE SWIVEL PIN, COCKS TOR

SWEATON WOODENSTONE GATE HANGER
(sx 699 732)

GATE HANGER, FRENCHBEER
(sx 675 857)

L-SHAPED GATEPOST

U-SHAPED GATEPOST

Dartmoor has a unique set of gate hangers or posts. Similar types can be seen in Cornwall, Isle of Purbeck and the Lake District, but as a set none surpass those of the Moor.

The finest is the woodenstone hanger, where a large holed stone projects over the edge of a wall allowing the extended upright of the gate to turn in the hole whilst pivoting, usually on a metal spigot set into a small hole in an earthfast stone. Holed hangers are quite common, though not many are still in their original position, some serving as gateposts, as at Frenchbeer.

All the other 'gates' utilize sets of poles inserted into slots. Where two sets of slots are utilized, those in one post would be deeper than the opposing set, allowing the bar to slide into the deeper slot before being swung into position and pushed back into the opposing slot. Each pole was held firm by a wedge.

The L-shaped slot only required the bar to follow the shape of the groove to be secure. The U-shape slotted gatepost called for the slot to get deeper along its length and required the post to lean backwards or called for the selection of a stone which would produce this attitude naturally. The bars, which were probably of differing lengths, descended in an arc downwards into the slot. Many posts have a slot cut in the top for an extra bar to be inserted.

Another type relied on a slot rebated into the edge. This must have been very inadequate, though Hansford Worth says a thin bar dropped through two iron rings would hold the gate bars in position. I know of only one example of this, in a wall on the west side of Bellever Tor, not far from Black's Newtake. Both posts are still in position though the gateway is infilled with dry stone walling. They stand much farther apart than would be normal, which might indicate they once formed part of the point-to-point races held thereabouts at the turn of the century.

EDGE-SLOT GATEPOST

EDGE-SLOT RETAINING BAR
(sx 646 758)

COMMON STILE
(sx 761 743)

The simplest stile was formed by setting stones to project from a wall,
sufficient to enable a person to step up, over, and down.

SHEEPFOLD
(sx 645 808)

The rearing of sheep was once a great industry. Vancouver states that 'some sheepyards have been constructed ... for sheltering their sheep, preserving their dung, and remedying the evils arising from the wetness of the land.' A Scotsman, introducing flocks of Scotch sheep, built a fold on the west flank of Stannon Tor. Its construction is very interesting for when standing inside and looking at the perimeter wall one sees tall vertical pillars set every few yards in the drystone wall. From outside none of these slabs can be detected.

There is the ruin of a building on the south side, while pens are picked out by three feet high posts on the other three sides. The top of these posts are grooved on the side facing the wall which may have held a pole leaning against the outer wall to support some form of covering, though none remains now.

Not long after it became derelict the fold was used for producing starch, though nothing seems to have come from this venture.

110

SHEEPSTELL
(sx 653 756)

There is a pound under Laughter Tor which might be a sheepstell. Pens were built that held a known number of sheep into which the shepherd could drive his flock. This pound has all the attributes of a stell being on the 'gentry' farm of Brimpts, whose occupiers were quite likely to import new ideas. The stell faces towards higher land unencumbered with any element to allow any dangerous build up of snow. The two large slabs set at right angles perhaps mark where hurdles divided off smaller pens for sorting out.

SHEEPWASH
(sx 666 753)

SHEEP DIP, TEIGNHEAD FARM

WOOL WEIGHT, 56lb – LITTLE BROOK
(sx 725 729)

In the era of short-woolled sheep, washing was carried out before shearing to remove any dirt and extraneous matter. A sheepwash was constructed by damming a stream to provide sufficient depth of quiet water where the sheep could be immersed and washed clean. On the right bank of the East Dart in Blackaton Mead, above Brimpts, are the remains of a sheepwash. All that can be seen now are the remains of pens and a narrow track down into the water. Sheep were also dipped against disease.

Once the fleece had been cut it was rolled up and put in the woolsack, the sack being weighed on a beam balance, granite blocks of known weight being used as measures.

GRINDSTONE
(sx 566 743)

Sheep shears needed constant sharpening, an old grindstone still exists at
Yellowmeade.

SHEEP CREEPS

The flock might not find sufficient food or space in the field provided so the
farmer would build an access point, known romantically as a sheep creep but
more correctly as a sheep hole, between fields or between a field and the
commons. Nearby should be a slab to close the access when required.

SHEEP LEAPS

The Devonport Leat was a long, unnatural obstacle to the freedom of sheep
to roam. To make crossing easier, stones were set to jut out from its banks.
These are commonly known as sheep leaps.

DITSWORTHY WARREN
(sx 584 663)

There are a feast of relics to be seen at Ditsworthy Warren: the warren
house, whose water supply was a leat brought through the house; the
skinning and packing sheds; the offal pool beside the entrance gate; a large
dog plat or kennel field with three kennels built into its walls. The wall itself
is topped with a lip to prevent the dogs from jumping out. Buries and
vermin traps abound on the warren itself, with odd pieces of vermin trap
being found around the warren house.

There are also supports for a grindstone beside the house, set over a
supply of water.

## VERMIN TRAPS

TRAP, DITSWORTHY

TRAP, DITSWORTHY

TRAP, LEGIS TOR
(sx 572 656)

TRAP, LEGIS TOR

The stoat and weasel preyed upon the rabbit, so the warrener devised a granite trap to destroy the menace. The trap was quite simple, consisting of an enclosed channel formed on one side with a single stone, the other side comprising two blocks. A large slab sat on top. At the limit of this capstone a groove was cut in each protruding side stone, down which a slate would drop, triggered when the vermin reached the mechanism set in the crack of the double-stoned side. Exactly how the mechanism worked must have varied as capstones can be found with one-to-four holes for this operation. To guide the vermin into the mouth of the trap the warrener built funnel walls in the shape of an X. He would of course use any convenient siting, so that we find the bank of a stream, tinner's burrow, or ancient reave utilized as guides to the trap.

## DOG KENNELS

### DITSWORTHY WARREN
(sx 584 663)

The warrener relied on his dogs to drive the rabbits into the catching nets. The dog plat is a large field at Ditsworthy and in its walls are three kennels, whereas at Trowlesworthy the small dog plat has no kennel but has steps outside to facilitate feeding.

The supposed dog kennel at Headland is also built into a wall, but is constructed like a mound to make it draught- and water-proof. It has an extremely neat interior finish. It is known that this kennel was later used as an ice house, and the quality of its finish indicates it was refurbished for this purpose, after it ceased to be used as a kennel.

HEADLAND WARREN
(sx 694 812)

## WARREN BOUNDS

HENTOR
(sx 584 644)

Two warrens, Hentor and Headland have their boundaries marked by engraved stones. Hentor's first marker is a large earthfast boulder with the letters HWB1 on its top surface, numbers 2, 3 and 4 are set stones. Stone 4, Dave Brewer tells me, has recently come to light and was found lying face down. Number 5 has yet to be discovered.

Headland Warren has a great variety of engravings, most like Bennett's Cross have the letters WB. One has the words WARREN BOUND, two have the single letter W. The one depicted here can be found close to the point where the southern boundary wall of the warren meets the Wallabrook. At one point the warren bound meets the North Bovey parish boundary and the WB stone here has the additional letter B. Close by another WB stone has the additional engraving of two sets of initials, AP and WN which some say are those of previous warreners.

WARREN BOUND, HEADLAND
(sx 695 817)

WB, HEADLAND
(sx 678 814)

W, HEADLAND
(sx 673 803)

WB + AP/WN, HEADLAND
(sx 697 808)

# 6
# THE DWELLING

The evidence we have from excavations of the Domesday Manor of Hundatora, the Houndtor medieval village, is that the first occupation (in times prior to the beginning of the tenth century), was for summer pasturage, with the erection of a simple shelter. This was followed by buildings made of turf, with an inner lining of wattle hurdling. Over five centuries of existence these dwellings slowly evolved, turf giving way to stone, and stone buildings being lengthened and enlarged. The new style became known as the longhouse.

Many dwelling sites were abandoned during the fourteenth century, due either to Black Death or to climatic deterioration, but the longhouse tradition continued.

The farmers of Stiniel, near Chagford, may have derived the name from Stone Hall, the first stone building in that district.

The importance the early highland community attached to their animals, cows and draft oxen, spilled over into their building requirements. The peasant farmer liked to keep his few possessions close to hand, so both man and beasts dwelt together under one roof. There is at Yardworthy, now used as a barn for cows, a building of this early period, the fourteenth century. The single room 32 feet × 14 feet is complete except for its roof.

Farms on Dartmoor are sparsely spread and may be single dwellings or small hamlets of three to five farmsteads. The choice of site was important, central to the holding, sheltered from the weather, and with a plentiful supply of good water.

The longhouse is protected from the prevailing wind by higher land, often surrounded by trees, planted for added protection.

The levelled site often has to follow the contour and is cut into the hillside, which gives added protection and strength. The dwelling is single-storey and built of granite blocks sometimes trimmed, sometimes massive in size. Double walls, large stones on the outside, smaller on the interior facing surfaces, the cavity filled with rubble, are as much as two feet or more thick. Traditionally the roof is thatched, replaced after centuries by slate or shingles.

The thatch varied. On primitive cottages turf and/or heather sufficed, but from field names we can deduce that rye and broom were used, rye first as an edible crop whereas broom was planted for the very purpose of cladding the roofs of longhouses, barns and corn ricks. The thatch was repaired and added to over the years. Crossing was able to record one roof over five feet thick.

The evolution from the single room was slow in the extreme, and changes were a matter of renovation and addition, rather than rebuilding.

If we look at the groundplan of Hundatora it is possible to determine an affluent order of society. The larger manor house for the lord or his deputy, three longhouse farms for the villeins and their cattle, and three one-roomed cottages.

The entrance to the longhouse, sufficient in size for both humans and animals, was protected by a porch of substantial proportions, wide enough for easy access and often accommodating seats on each side where the family could sit on warm summer evenings, there being little light indoors from lack of windows.

The first change was to build a partition between the two halves, the down-slope end being the cattle quarters which had a drain down the centre and often a dung door, for removing soiled bedding. At first the partition was a simple affair and did not reach the thatch; later it was a substantial stone wall dividing the dwelling into two parts, with a second door inserted into the wall opposite the porch to form a cross passage.

The inner side of the new axial wall contained a new hearth, with a large tapering chimney above. The sides of the hearth were made of large slabs of granite with a massive lintel. A beam, often of wood, was positioned across the chimney from which the cooking utensils were hung and above this might be placed a hook for curing bacon.

The thatch was supported by crucks or couples, a local term, self-explanatory when a matching pair would be cut from the same tree. They were spaced approximately eight feet apart, or half a yoke (a full yoke of oxen was taken as sixteen feet). As tie beams were seldom employed, additional strengtheners of stone were sometimes placed against the outside wall to hold it in, but this was done only when required.

The floors were usually of compacted earth, occasionally paving was used in the cross passage.

It is not easy to categorize building changes in terms of dates and order, but the next major change was for the longhouse to grow up. It was to remain one room wide, and is still so today, all rooms having to be entered from the preceding one. By lengthening the living quarters a division was made for an inner room, the dairy, later known as the parlour. Above this an additional room was added. The extra height also allowed a tallet, as the hayloft was known, to subdivide the animal quarters.

Stairs to the upper room were generally circular, of granite or oak built into a specially thickened part of the wall. A variation would be for granite blocks to protrude from the wall.

At the beginning of the seventeenth century there was a great upsurge in new building. The main purpose was to increase the size of the living accommodation. The new houses had an enlarged porch, over which a room was added, used as a store for wool, grain or apples. This new style of building is quite easily recognisable, and often an arch was constructed over the entrance, engraved with the date and initials of the owner.

At this period the cattle were provided with a separate entrance, and much later were moved to a building of their own.

The old longhouse was updated in a similar fashion, rooms were built over the great hall, and additional rooms could be added as lean-tos or outshots. The outshot became the dairy and the dairy the parlour. When used as a kitchen or scullery they are often referred to as the backhouse. The introduction of a separate place for cooking, the kitchen, was not within the farmhouse but in a barn.

An inventory of the rectory at Lydford from the early seventeenth century paints a clear picture: 'Imprimis the hall and a parler [parlour], with chamber over the parler, the entry with a chamber over the entry, on [one] buttery, a barne, on [one] cowe house and a stable, with a little kytchin at the end of yt'.

It was further described some sixty years later in 1680, by the then rector: 'The houses there unto belonging is a hall and parlour and two Chambers, the Hall and parlour paved underfoote, on [one] deary and on [one] woodhouse earthen floore. The outhouses is a Barne, a chitching, stable, and Linney house with earthen floores. The walls of all the said houses are of stone.'

A later rector, describing this as a 'hovel', demolished the lot and rebuilt on the same site.

There are many other innovations within the general development of the Dartmoor longhouse. With the building of the axial wall and hearth, a bread oven and salt shelf were inserted at the back or to one side of the hearth. Like the kitchen another 'little room' started its life as a separate external building, the privy. At Chittleford at the back of the farmhouse can be found a disused double-seated lavatory, it was built of small granite blocks and erected over a stream for continuous flushing. A stone faced embankment leads to the toilet seats.

One of the few garderobes on Dartmoor is to be found on the first floor of the 'Upper Hall' at Neadon, near Manaton. This building is of extreme interest for it is the only example of the shippen being downstairs with living quarters above, reached originally by a flight of stone steps. Though this building probably dates from the sixteenth century a similar design can be seen in the Bayeux Tapestry where Earl Harold is depicted eating a meal in such a house before his ill-fated voyage to France. Though long used as a barn, Neadon Upper Hall has now been restored as a dwelling house.

THE PORCH, SANDERS, LETTAFORD
(sx 702 841)

The Dartmoor longhouse has been with us for a thousand years and its
enduring quality is epitomised by the simplicity and indestructible
appearance of its entrance.

'MANOR' LONGHOUSE, HOUNDTOR MEDIEVAL VILLAGE
(sx 746 787)

This deserted village is recorded in the Domesday Book as Hundatora, held by Tavistock Abbey. It existed for about five hundred years, its life ended either by the Black Death or from a deterioration in the climate at that time.

The remains on the ground give a very good impression of a small, compact community, showing the layout of the longhouse, the outshot addition and barn. One can clearly determine an affluent order of society. The larger manor house for the lord, three longhouse farms for the villeins and their cattle, and three one-roomed cottages.

YARDWORTHY PORCH
(sx 679 852)

YARDWORTHY WINDOW

Outbuildings are frequently very interesting, in many cases originally being dwellings. A barn at Yardworthy was originally a single room dwelling. The porch, offset to one end and sufficient for cattle to enter with ease, still has the primitive pivot hole at the top from which the door was hung. The window at the rear has pivot holes showing it was never glazed only shuttered. Note that it is level with the ground, an example of contouring the site.

127

CHOLWICH TOWN DOORWAY

CHOLWICH TOWN WINDOW
(sx 587 619)

Two barns at Cholwich Town, a farm that has been in existence from at least the thirteenth century, have evidences of very neat doors and windows which could indicate their former use as a dwelling.

## LONGHOUSES

OLLSBRIM
(sx 688 735)

BONEHILL
(sx 726 776)

STINIEL
(sx 706 855)

The rear view of Ollsbrim provides an excellent example of the simplicity of the longhouse. It appears to hug the ground, running downhill from the dwelling to the animal quarters. Updated in the seventeenth century, a large, dated porch with a room over was added.

Granite quoins, corner stones, are often disproportionate to the rest. Sometimes ashlar (trimmed) blocks are used or, as at Stiniel, the rear wall is made up of very large slabs.

YEO
(sx 551 669)

This is the finest specimen of the changed style of dwelling, introduced in the seventeenth century. The quality of its workmanship would seem to indicate the owner was a person of some standing and wealth. The porch is initialled I.W. (John Woodcombe), and dated 1610.

## DATED DOORWAYS

YEO
(sx 551 669)

BERRYDOWN
(sx 667 879)

ABB'S HOUSE
(sx 656 639)

The dated and sometimes initialled arched doorway came into vogue at the beginning of the seventeenth century. Yeo, 1610 is among the earliest. Berrydown, another very substantial manor farm, has a porch, dated 1655 and initialled I.R.
A more recent example is to be found in the ruins of Abb's House, C.B. 1809.

SANDERS, LETTAFORD
(sx 702 841)

The hamlet of Lettaford was first recorded in 1244 as Lottreford. In the nineteenth century the three farms were known as Sanders and Natsworthy Littaford, Southmeads Littaford, and Higher Littaford and Black Sticks.

As the front elevation is approached, one is struck by its strength and beauty, albeit that the wall area above the carefully cut and trimmed ashlar blocks of the shippen is of rough stone walling, giving the effect that the farm might have fallen into ruin and some of the ashlar blocks removed before rebuilding. However, it is likely that the farm was originally built in this manner.

The Dartmoor farmer was a proud, thrifty man, even vain, and it is not uncommon that great attention was paid to the 'first view'. A similar approach to West Combe sees the ashlar blocks forming the corners of the shippen with rough stone walling above, into which is set a very attractive dung door.

WEST COMBE
(sx 709 825)

The longhouse was built up rather than cut into the hillside. It is said that the cross passage was set along the line of the Mariners Way and the sailors would pass through on their way to the next port. The doorway with its excellent masonry is a most striking feature.

## SANDERS, LETTAFORD

DOOR DURNS

Sanders, Lettaford shows many of the features described, especially renovations over many years. The shippen is largely in its original condition. On either side of the drain are manger stones, the posts let into these would have been attached to the floor of the tallet. Some of the beams which supported the tallet floor are still in place and are set into the rough stone walling of the inner skin. The roof of the shippen is a fine example of the carpenter's and sawyer's craft, no branch was wasted, odd shapes were utilized to the full, and the ingenuity of the builder put to the test.

In 1978 Sanders was restored by the Landmark Trust and is now preserved as an outstanding example of a Dartmoor Longhouse. The photographs here show the building before restoration.

REAR EXIT

In the previous photograph, note how the wood door durns at the rear of the porch match the stonework of the outer doorway. The cross passage leads direct to a rear door, which gave access to a small barn, this too is fine ashlar building, a little spoilt by the cutting of slots for the bars of a gate. Its matching style would seem to indicate an age contemporary with the dwelling. Upstairs, an original cruck can be seen peeping through the plaster.

In the shippen can be seen the original beam which supported the tallet floor. Below are lines of manger stones, the footsteps in which the manger posts stood, with the other end being attached to the tallet floor.

BARN

CRUCK

TALLET RAFTER

MANGER STONES

LETTAFORD SHIPPEN
(sx 702 841)

The woodwork supporting the shippen roof visually explains the local name
'couples' given to crucks, cut as they are by dividing the selected trunk and
branch into two.

BEETOR LINTEL
(sx 711 844)

The mason chose a very large piece of granite to form the lintel over the hearth and to support the chimney wall above. Its disproportion to the stones above is very common. In some farms the lintel was of equal size but of wood. Beetor farmhouse was destroyed by fire in the 1940s.

UPPACOTT
(sx 701 728)

A raised cruck supports the roof of the shippen at Uppacott. Note that the
wood cover to the cross passage never reached the roof.

BREAD OVEN

SALT SHELF

CHIMNEY

The great fireplace of Dunstone Court/Manor holds several treasures. The bread oven is an excellent sample of the mason's art, the near-perfect round stone base and matching walling, leaning in to form a perfect dome. The fireplace also has a salt shelf built to keep dry the salt, normally bought as a block. The narrowing chimney reaches up to the sky, spanned by a (wooden!) beam which held the irons to support the kettle, pots and pans above the fire.

CHITTLEFORD PRIVY
(sx 722 756)

The little room built out over a stream for continual flushing, with its
double seat for extra convenience.

### NEADON UPPER HALL
(sx 751 825)

Pevsner describes, 'Neadon Farm with a separate ashlar chapel of c1500'. He may be right as to the date, but though other writers also refer to it being a chapel, there is no traceable connection with a religious house. The wood tracery of one of the upper windows is the only apparent basis for this assumption.

This two storey building with the shippen on the ground floor and dwelling above is unique on Dartmoor. It has some marvellous woodwork, apart from the craftmanship of the window, two doors are exquisite, the lower with its extra width for animals and the upper formerly reached by a flight of stone steps. On the upper floor is a garderobe.

The photographs show Neadon 'Upper Hall' prior to its recent restoration as a dwelling house by the late Vernon Hunt.

142

NEADON, WINDOW TRACERY

NEADON, UPPER DOORWAY

NEADON, SHIPPEN DOOR

# 7
# THE
# FARMYARD

Adjacent to the longhouse were sited a range of interesting buildings and facilities that make up the Dartmoor farmstead. Commonest amongst the granite artefacts is the trough, which comes in all shapes and sizes, single and double, round and rectangular.

Chemical fertilizers did not arrive on the farming scene until the middle of the nineteenth century, so the farmer used the fertilizers he had, the manure from his animals and the ash from his fire (sand and seaweed were also used). Ash from the fire was taken out at night and placed in a little building known as the ash house, to prevent sparks from reaching the thatch. The most common design was a small round building, with a hatch facing the house and a larger door opposite through which the ash was removed. Most had a stone-clad, domed roof. Rectangular ash houses followed in the nineteenth century. Lime was increasingly used as a fertilizer, and numerous lime kilns can be found on the edges of the moor. None appear to exist on the moor proper, though among field names 'kiln close' or 'kiln meadow' are quite common.

Vancouver in his discourse on the peasant farmer reports: 'it is common practice among them, on marriage to give their wives, what is called pin-money: this consists of poultry, pigs and the whole produce of the dairy; with which supply the wife is expected to clothe and (exclusive of bread, corn and other vegetables) support the whole household.'

## The dairy

After 'bucketing' as milking was called, the fresh milk was taken to the dairy and strained through muslin into a cloamen pan. After standing it was scalded. Once scalded the milk and cream were allowed to cool, and the cream skimmed off. Scald cream or clotted (clouted) cream is still much in demand as 'real Devonshire cream' by the thousands of visitors who annually flock to the moors for their holidays. But the farmer's wife of yesteryear would turn most of it into butter by hand.

Keeping milk, cream and butter in hot weather was a problem, but the local DIY farmer-mason had ways of solving the problem. At South Harton there is a substantial barn, at one end of which is a dairy where churns stood on a channelled granite shelf. Along this the farmer diverted a small stream to keep the milk cool.

At Chittleford there is a domestic butter cooler. Built into the wall, which forms the edge of the embankment leading to the privy, is a small opening, the base of which is a V-shaped channel. Above this is mounted a flat slate shelf. Water was diverted to flow along the channel to keep butter placed on the shelf from melting.

While camping at Barewalls above the Wallabrook before the Second World War the author remembers obtaining water from a well in which a shelf had been fitted level with the water. Here would stand jugs and bowls of milk and cream.

Along with cream and butter, the farmer's wife would also make cheese. In this process the curds and whey would be placed in muslin on a grooved stone and pressed until all the whey, the surplus liquid, had been extracted. The granite bases for this operation are still to be found on the moor.

Though it cannot be considered as archaeologically important at the present time, the churn platform, once so common, will now sink into oblivion. In the days when surplus milk was collected in churns, farmers built platforms at suitable points on the nearest public road, to exchange full churns for empty ones.

## Pigeons

There appears to be not a single instance of a dovecot, pigeon or culver house on upland Dartmoor. One can see on the sides of houses and barns where stones have been deliberately left out so that convenient nesting sites were available for this additional food supply. Pigeons were also reared as a supplement to fish on Fridays, and for their eggs.

Harrison wrote at the end of the sixteenth century 'Our tame foule are such (for the most part) as are common both to vs and to other countries, as cocks, hens, geese, duckes, peacocks, of Inde, pigeons, now an hurtfull foule by reason of their multitudes, and number of houses dailie erected for their increase (which the bowres of the countrie call in scorne almes houses, and dens of theeues, and such like) whereof there is great plentie in everie farmers yard.'

There is at Bagtor, in the Parish of Ilsington a particularly delightful old barn, part of a sweep of buildings. The wall of the barn is studded with nesting holes.

## Geese and Pigs

Both geese and ducks have their own houses on Dartmoor. The goosehouse is always positioned so that the geese can give the alarm should any intruder pass by. Anyone who has experienced passing too close to geese will know the immediate response this brings.

Vancouver observed that the native hog of the county grows to a large size, and when fed on a 'mixture of two-thirds of boiled or steamed potatoes, and one-third pease and barley ground in equal quantities into meal, well mixed together' gives excellent results. I doubt if the cottager went to all that trouble for it was customary to raise a pig which fended for itself, and what it could garner at the kitchen door.

The round pig trough is very common and often mistaken as the base stone of a cider mill. An interesting feature which can be seen at Kingshead above Widecombe, and at Ford near Manaton, is the use of a rectangular trough built into the thickness of the pigsty wall to facilitate feeding without entering the sty itself.

## Potatoes

Potatoes were an exceedingly good and valuable crop on the east side of the moor. In the eighteenth century, Chagford and Moretonhampstead district had a monopoly in potato cultivation, and produce was taken to Two Bridges to be sold to Plymouth and Tavistock dealers. Donn's map of Devon designates 'The Saracen's Head' at Two Bridges as the site of the potato market.

Robert Burnard states that 'in many of the southern and western districts the cultivation was severely handicapped, for leases of only a century since forbade the growth of potatoes beyond what was absolutely necessary for the use of the tenant and his family.' It is not surprising to find in these south-western districts of Dartmoor, caves, dug into the growan for the storage of potatoes.

## Beekeeping

Another and very ancient aspect of farming on Dartmoor was beekeeping. There is a reference in the Domesday Book (Exon) for a tithe collection wherein five beekeepers of Lustleigh paid seven sextaries (sesters) of honey. At that time the King's Kitchen Master held lands in the district, honey being the only available sweetener.

William Harrison, five hundred years later says, 'Our honie also is taken and reputed to be the best, because it is harder, better wrought, and clenlier vesselled vp'.

There are two types of shelter on Dartmoor associated with beekeeping. One Hansford Worth refers to as a shelter, the other which Brother Adam of Buckfast Abbey, an authority on beekeeping on Dartmoor, calls bee boles. These latter are much older, and those in a collapsed mediaeval wall at Buckfast Abbey are said to be the oldest in Britain.

## Dogs

Polwhele attributes to a Mr Whitaker the statement that the Britons of Dumnonia 'had beehives near the manfions of the chiefs, and near their farm-houses', and adds 'the houfe was guarded by the British Maftiff'. Harrison bases his account of British dogs on Strabo's views which were that this mastiff was a ferocious creature, frequently crossed with lions and tigers.

No Dartmoor farmer would keep a dog which could not pay its way and, alongside the ubiquitous sheepdog, the most likely dog to be kept was some form of spaniel. It is noticeable that the kennel is placed in a strategic position, similar to the goosehouse.

## Corn and cider

Once the farmer had harvested his corn he had to prepare it for grinding. First it was threshed and then cleaned. Possibly the cross passage was built with its opposing doors deliberately to assist in this work, for once threshed, at the threshold, it was cleaned by winnowing. The straw was removed and the rest gathered up and tossed in a draught of air, the heavy grains fell vertically while the dust and chaff was blown away. On some Dartmoor farms a windstrew was constructed for this purpose, a raised platform out in the open where winnowing could be carried out. One such at Longstone, above sixteen feet square, has steps for mounting to the top, one of which has cut in its surface JE 1640.

Originally threshing was carried out by a man wielding a flail, or in the Devon vernacular, thrashel. This was superseded by the threshing machine.

Before the age of steam, setting aside manpower, the power sources available to operate machinery were water and beasts. Water was used to propel great wheels, while beasts, mainly horses, trod an endless circular course, turning a large wooden spur-wheel. A succession of gears and shafts from the spur-wheel provided the power to drive machinery which separated the corn from the straw. The horse gear was housed in a roundhouse, though hexagonal and rectangular buildings were also used.

The building used for cider making is commonly called a poundhouse, the apples being crushed by a large granite wheel which rotated round a stone trough. Once the apples had been crushed the 'mock' was placed in a simple press above a grooved base stone through which the juice would run into a trough or kieve. Pressure was brought to bear using a block of granite with a ring in the top, manipulated by a large beam.

Later, apples were crushed using horsepower to turn either granite rollers or fluted iron rollers. The press, like a vertical vice, moved on two metal threads operated by turning a wheel.

Another magnificent but simple instrument found on Dartmoor farms is the stone roller. Many now lie broken, some abandoned among the weeds and bracken, but plenty are still in use. Vancouver wrote 'The common one and two horse-rollers, with heavy granite or moorstone rollers, of from 5 to 8 feet in length and of proportionate diameter, are very generally used.' Similar rollers can also be seen scaled down for use in gardens.

One other common piece of stonework is the upping stock. As people were heavily reliant on horses, a set of steps was built as an aid for a rider to mount his horse. Any natural rock might also be left in position if it would serve the same purpose.

Finally there are many objects on the Dartmoor farm which defy explanation. For instance in the side of a barn at West Combe is a trough over which a neat arch has been built. It may only be a feeding place, but it was even suggested that it was an early font!

TEIGNHEAD, FARMYARD
(sx 635 844)

Ruined farmyard of Teignhead Farm. The commonest utensil made from granite is the trough, this example might be a tinner's mould from the nearby Blacksmith's Shop blowing house. It is not really the correct shape for a tinner's mould, though a farmer wanting a trough would enlarge such a convenient object. There is evidence of a test mould on one edge of the trough.

ROUND TROUGH, HEADLAND
(sx 694 812)

Troughs come in all shapes and sizes as can be seen at Headland. Troughs being fed by a leat indicate the source of the original water supply to a dwelling and are known as dipping troughs. At Routrundle the leat, having fed the trough, then crosses the yard in a paved channel to feed a sheep dip. Troughs used in cider making were known as kieves.

Two troughs at Sortridge have dates 1666, 1667, embossed on their surface.

RECTANGULAR TROUGH, HEADLAND

DOUBLE TROUGH, HEADLAND

DIPPING TROUGH, ROUTRUNDLE
(sx 555 717)

KIEVE, MEAVY
(sx 540 672)

DATED TROUGH, SORTRIDGE
(sx 550 710)

## ASH HOUSES

ASH HOUSE, FORD
(sx 733 812)

The first ash houses were round, the hatch facing the house with a door facing into the field. A very large, possibly the largest ash house is at Ford, Manaton. It is topped by the cap of a staddle stone, a later adornment. At West Combe the ash house is built into the hedge, on the far side of a road, not an uncommon position. The later rectangular ash house has no hatch and a flat roof. The Frenchbeer ash house seems to be an evolution between the two, being rectangular but with a corbelled roof, now capped with layer of cement. The Babeny ash house is also built into a wall, but has only a door. In its setting on the far side of a stroll running through enclosures towards Laughter Hole Steps, it could possibly be a goose house.

ASH HOUSE, FORD

ASH HOUSE, WEST COMBE
(sx 709 825)

ASH HOUSE, FRENCHBEER
(sx 675 858)

ASH HOUSE, BABENY
(sx 672 752)

LIME KILN, DREWSTEIGNTON
(sx 730 914)

The first chemical fertilizer available on Dartmoor was lime. Outcrops of limestone (culm) appear at several places on the edge of the moor and this was burnt in kilns to produce lime. In the first instance the stone was brought onto the moor by packhorse and reduced in kilns on the farms, for we find among the field names kiln close, kiln meadow, but no remains of kilns survive. Later, large kilns were built next to the quarries. Several can be seen at Drewsteignton though these may be subject to erosion by the re-use of the quarries for road stone. The labourers' cottages, except for a lone chimney standing against the elements, have already collapsed.

WATER DAIRY, SOUTH HARTON
(sx 768 822)

COOLER, CHITTLEFORD
(sx 722 756)

RESERVOIR, SOUTH HARTON

A farmer at South Harton kept his milk cool by standing churns or buckets of milk on a grooved granite shelf along which he directed a stream of water. Enterprisingly he then fed the water to a large granite trough outside the back door to his house. The stream then flows across the farmyard and into a reservoir set in one end of a large barn. The only entrance to the reservoir is over the outlet which is a slight groove in a large trimmed stone set under a very neat arch.

The farmer at Chittleford directed a flow of water under a slate shelf upon which butter and cream were kept cool.

155

CHURN PLATFORM, RIDDON
(sx 680 767)

The milk churn platform is not an archaeological antiquity. Churn collections from farms continued until 1978. It was the responsibility of the farmer to take the churns to the nearest public road, where he had built a platform at a height which enabled the collector to move the full churn onto the back of the collecting vehicle. They are included here for such platforms are becoming derelict and overgrown, and will fade into obscurity.

Apart from cream, the farmer's wife would make cheese. The curds and whey were placed in a muslin square, the corners tied together, and squeezed between a base stone which was grooved with a lip to facilitate drainage, and a heavy block lowered on top. Cheese press bases are invariably round, but at a later date a ratchet and screw exerted pressure in a rectangular box. Was the base stone then square? A base stone built high into a wall at Beetor Farm seems more rectangular than round, but it is difficult to get close enough to be sure.

CHEESE PRESS BASE, BEETOR FARM
(sx 711 844)

CHEESE PRESS BASE, SHEEPSTOR CHURCHYARD
(sx 560 677)

BARN AT BAGTOR BARTON
(sx 766 753)

GOOSEHOUSE, BEETOR FARM
(sx 711 844)

DETAIL OF PIGEON NEST HOLES

There appears to be no culver house (pigeon loft) on Dartmoor. On many farms nest holes have been left for the convenience of the birds to breed. The best example is at Bagtor Barton. The façade of this barn is a delight and a close-up reveals this superb example of rough stone walling, showing the care taken in selecting stones.

159

DUCK HOUSES, FORD
(sx 709 825)

Most goosehouses appear to be built under steps, for example at Ellimore near Lustleigh. Here the goosehouse is under the steps leading to a small granary, similarly at Gratton (Meavy) and Neadon (Manaton). But at Beetor in the farmyard is a detached goosehouse, built of granite blocks. The rear is covered with an earth mound forming one wall of the yard, the other sides being formed by buildings, including the original longhouse. An interesting feature is that the pond that is directly in front of the goosehouse to prevent vermin from access to the geese at night. Goosehouses always seem to have been positioned so that the birds could raise the alarm at the appearance of any intruder.

When the wall at the back of the farmyard at Ford was built, two compartments were constructed into and behind it, below ground level. The entrances, about eighteen inches square, open out to give a space four to five feet square and about two feet high. Granite blocks form the roof with three or four feet of earth above. Inset into the granite door-framing can be seen the ironwork for fixing doors. Mark Beeson, who lived at Ford, recalls that they were used for ducks, until a badger got in and destroyed the occupants.

PIGSTIES, FORD
(sx 733 812)

FEEDING TROUGH, EXTERIOR

FEEDING TROUGH, INTERIOR

BOAR PEN

Pigs were commonly kept on farms and by most cottagers. At Ford the pig pens opened out onto their own yard, which had two round troughs at one end and a boar pen at the other. An interesting but not uncommon feature are the feeding troughs of the pens which are built into the width of the wall, with the lip just clear of the pen floor. Because the land outside is at a much lower level feeding takes place conveniently at waist-level so that the farmer did not have to disturb a farrowing sow.

POTATO CAVE, LEATHER TOR FARM
(sx 569 699)

Potatoes were stored on many farms in underground chambers cut into the
growan. These were dry, cool and frostproof.

BEE BOLES, FORD
(sx 733 812)

Bee boles, the protected shelf on which the hives stood, are quite common. There is an exceptional set at Beetor, with massive granite lintels. Also here, inside a barn, is a niche in the wall, thought to be a 'skep' hole where the straw hives were kept in winter. There is an excellent set at Ford and, though much decayed, the oldest are said to be at Buckfast Abbey. A shelter at Brownberry, of a more recent date, had a wooden door. Unfortunately the roof slab has been broken and collapsed inward. Somewhere between the boles and shelter in date, are two recesses in the ruins of Yes Tor Farm possibly connected with beekeeping. These look out onto a small private courtyard.

Harrison (c 1590) says 'Our hives are made comonlie of rie straw, and wadled about with bramble quarters: but some make them of wicker, and cast them over with claie'. He goes on to say they are set so 'that they may stand drie and without danger of the mouse and moth.'

BEE BOLE, BUCKFAST
(sx 741 674)

SHELTER, BROWNBERRY
(sx 647 745)

BEE BOLES(?), YES TOR FARM
(sx 563 727)

DOG KENNEL, BEETOR FARM
(sx 711 844)

Four or five slabs made a shelter for a dog, positioned to guard the homestead. At Beetor Farm it stood between the house and the yard, the yard being given double protection by the geese, housed on the far side. The entrance to Crazywell Farm has a handsome shelter, which from its position by the farm gate, is a dog kennel, suitable for a spaniel. Hemery records this as a cooler, although from its exposed position to the sun (by the gate), seems unlikely.

DOG KENNEL, CRAZYWELL FARM
(sx 581 702)

RICK BASE, HUCKEN TOR FARM
(sx 549 742)

When the corn was cut it was stacked in a rick, the base being made of faggots, bundles of twigs, laid either on a low, flat mound or on a series of upright stones, to keep the corn clear of the wet ground and away from vermin. At this point it was unthreshed. Once threshed, the grains and chaff would be gathered up and separated by being tossed in a current of air, the heavy grains falling to the ground, but dust and chaff floating further afield. The Dartmoor farmer built a platform, the windstrew, to aid this action. The windstrew at Longstone has a set of steps to the top, one inscribed JE 1640 (John Elford).

WINDSTREW, LONGSTONE
(sx 557 685)

ROUNDHOUSE, FRENCHBEER
(sx 675 868)

It was in the roundhouse that the threshing machinery was housed. Horses
provided the power, walking an endless circular path, hence the name.

ROUNDHOUSE, BAGTOR BARTON
(sx 766 753)

HORSE GEAR, BATWORTHY FARM
(sx 715 853)

The horse gear comprised an axle, set vertically in a stone footstep, forming the centre of a large spur-wheel which turned the mechanism through a series of cog wheels. The horse was harnessed to an arm below the spur-wheel. Note in the example at Batworthy Farm all the spur-wheel and cogs are made of wood, even to being held together by wooden pins. There was not much room and the farmer there recalled how sparks would fly when the horse's shoes struck the wall as it went by. Here the operation was for crushing apples which were fed from the loft above, between the fluted metal rollers of the tumbler mill, sliding down the shute into the waiting receptacle.

SHAFT

TUMBLER MILL

CIDER MILL, LONGSTONE
(sx 557 685)

In ancient times apples were pounded into pulp by the weight of a stone wheel, pivoting on a central axle, and rotated by a horse walking round the huge, granite trough-like base. Some mills have sloping internal edges and are made up of two halves strapped together by iron bars. Unless they are very large most round troughs with a central projecting knob are in fact only pig troughs, mills are rare.

The pulp was placed on a round flat stone, with grooves which lead to a lip. A heavy granite block manipulated by a lever exerted pressure on the pulp, squeezing the juice out, which flowed via the grooves and lip into a waiting kieve or trough.

At Batworthy Farm the pulp was placed between layers of straw under the press and squeezed. About two tons of apples could be pressed free of juice at any one time. The base of the press is raised for the convenience of allowing the juice to flow into vats or barrels. The original wood screw press was of a giant size but, after 1800, metal threaded screws were introduced, an iron wheel being used to operate the mechanism.

CIDER PRESS, BATWORTHY FARM
(sx 715 853)

CIDER PRESS BASE, MEAVY
(sx 540 672)

KIEVES, LONGSTONE

CIDER PRESS BASE, LONGSTONE

STONE ROLLER, NATTADON
(sx 706 869)

UPPING STOCK, OLD INN,
WIDECOMBE

RUDE STONE ROLLER, TEIGNHEAD FARM
(sx 635 844)

UPPING STOCK, WIDECOMBE
(sx 718 767)

One sees on many Dartmoor farms granite agricultural rollers, some broken, some abandoned, with weeds and bracken already submerging this magnificent but simple instrument. A crude granite roller, probably made locally by hand, can be seen on Teignhead Farm, re-used as a gate post.

There abound on farms and in the villages mounting blocks, more correctly upping stocks, a series of steps apparently going nowhere, to aid the horseman to mount. There are steps outside the vicarage at Widecombe, and in the same village, outside the Old Inn, a piece of bedrock granite was deliberately left to assist the victualler's customers.

TROUGH, WEST COMBE
(sx 709 825)

TROUGH, MUSCOVEY DUCK

A neat trough set into the wall of a small barn at West Combe, protected by
an arch, seems out of place. It is difficult to define its use. It stands beside the
Mariners Way and travellers may have used it. Someone obviously knew
what to use it for!

# 8
# THE VILLAGE

The village is the pivot of a rural society. In the lowland zone of Dartmoor the farmhouses are centred within the village bounds, but in the highland zone, with the exception of the glebe farm, they are 'out of town' and scattered, many at a considerable distance from the centre point.

As examples we here concentrate on the village of Widecombe-in-the-Moor and the hamlet of Ponsworthy, just over two miles away, in the valley of the West Webburn.

The phrase 'out of town' may seem a little incongruous when dealing with a Parish whose population for most of its history has been less than a thousand, but Widecombe Town is the name given to one of the six manors which form the present parish. It is frequently referred to in old documents as Higher Town, and a small cluster of dwellings, far down the valley of the Webburn, formerly Christians Hays, is still known as Lower Town.

It was in the village that were found the seat of government and subsidiary services to the community.

In 1857 at Ponsworthy, John Tollick was the miller and baker, and Charles Warren a shoemaker. On one side of the river at Lincheford, John Caunter was a carpenter and wheelwright, while on the other side at Fernhill we find William Beard, shoemaker, Thomas Turner, thatcher, John Warren, tailor, John Warren, mason, and John Withycombe, carpenter.

Residing at Widecombe was a miller, baker, blacksmith, innkeeper (victualler), and based on the Church we find the offices of church warden, constable, waywarden, and overseer of the poor.

The people of one parish lived similar lives to any of the others found on Dartmoor, but the people of Widecombe were fortunate that due to absentee landlords they were able to exert a large degree of self-control. This they achieved under a system of local government, through which all parishioners had to carry out compulsory duties for the good of all, under the directions of wardens.

The office of warden was very demanding. It must have taken a great deal of time and was unpaid – a likely reason for the appointed person holding office only for one year. To ease matters the parish was divided into quarters, and the number of wardens appropriately proportioned: two church-wardens, four overseers of the poor, four highway surveyors, and a constable.

## The Church and Churchyard

Quite rightly Widecombe church is known as the Cathedral of the Moor. Dedicated to St Pancras, it has been renovated on several occasions but basically it has survived intact for more than five hundred years.

Widecombe itself cannot be identified from entries in the Domesday Book, its list of rectors begins with 'John (unknown) 1253'. The earliest documentation referring to the church is Bishop Bronscombe's *Ordinacio de Lideford*, 1260, which states that the tenants of Babeny and Pizwell should worship and receive all sacraments in life and death at Widecombe. This edict took the church's influence outside its own borders and into the Forest.

A document of 1283 concerns an acre of land adjacent to

the 'Mother Church' of the Parish which was sold to the Dean and Chapter of Exeter.

In 1406, John Shillingford, Canon of Exeter, expressed in his will the wish to be buried in the Chapel of St Katherine, in the parish church at Widecombe, next to his mother.

There is, therefore, unequivocal evidence of a thirteenth century church at Widecombe. The church house was built early in the sixteenth century, about 1538. A study of its masonry and a comparison to that of the church tower, reveal similarities that make it fairly safe to state that they were built in the same period. The tower itself is therefore a later addition to the church.

Widecombe is a typical cruciform church with its roof supported on octagonal monolith piers of granite with funnel shaped caps and chamfered bases, completely unadorned, as are the chamfered arches above. Interestingly the arches in the north and south chantries are of moulded wood.

The tower, the commanding feature its creators intended, rises 135 feet from the ground. It was too big for the existing church so the roof of the nave and that of the north and south aisles had to be raised to accommodate the arch within the older church, it also overlaps the original windows on either side.

It has been said that the tinners built the tower in tribute to their good fortune, but the coinage returns for Ashburton in June 1523 show payments by 'St Pancras of Wythicombe' and 'St Pancras of Wethycomb'. This indicates that at about the time when the tower was built there was a Church Guild or investment in the tin industry which may itself have funded the building of the tower.

The church roof is of the cradle type with many of its original bosses, carved and painted. During a major renovation original wall plates, depicting heads, the white hart of Richard II, and a griffin were destroyed.

The famous storm, a tornado which hit the church during the Sunday afternoon service on 21 October 1638, killed four people and injured a great many more; two of these are buried in the nave. The north-east pinnacle was thrown down and it fell again, due to an earthquake, in 1752. All traces of this damage were recently eradicated when the tower was repointed.

An old churchyard is always of interest, the words on gravestones being informative – occasionally vulgar or humorous. Rowe recorded this social comment from a stone at Ashburton which he says had recently been destroyed:

> Here I lie at the Chancel door,
> Here I lie because I'm poor,
> The further in the more you pay
> Here lie I as warm as they.

At Widecombe, before 1762, those who could afford the price – 6/8d for an adult, 3/4d for a child – could be buried in the church.

There are 277 memorials in Widecombe churchyard, many of granite. Some have been moved and many are to more than one member of a family. The records show that between 1560 and 1801, 4044 burials took place and it is reasonable to assume that the area round the church had been the parish graveyard at least from the incumbency of the first rector in 1253.

In ancient times the dead were wrapped in a shroud and carried on a bier, a simple stretcher. The dead from Dartmeet, Hexworthy and the farms in that direction had to be carried up Yartor Hill, and on the way the party would rest at the rock now known as the Coffin Stone. It is adorned with a series of crosses and initials.

## Milling and Baking

The reducing of corn to flour is one of man's oldest occupations. It would be very satisfying if we could trace its development on Dartmoor from earliest times down to the present day. The oldest method was by pounding, and there are stones on the moor with small cups in their surface which suggest where this might have been done. The pounding method was followed by grain rubbers, the process of reduction by rubbing with one stone on another with a circular motion. From then it was simple evolution to the saddlestone which involved a backwards and forwards motion, causing greater wear at the centre of the stone and thereby forming the saddle shape. Rubbers and saddlestones have both been found on the moor. These methods died out in the Iron Age.

The rotary handmill, correctly known as a quern, was probably introduced by the Romans. The Saxon peasantry gradually introduced the era of grinding the village's collective corn into flour. The quern would produce only enough flour to satisfy a small household. The medieval water mill on the other hand demanded a captive audience. Each manor had a mill of its own and all the lord's tenants had to use it. Where possible querns were destroyed to ensure that this occurred.

To stand amidst the magnificent machinery of a mill when in operation, to hear the rumble and creak as the wheels turn, to feel the hot meal as it flows into waiting sacks is an unforgettable experience. Alas none of these mills have worked on the moor since 1938.

Crossing says 'In 1302 or 1303 the holders of the tenements in the Forest built a mill at Babeny at their own cost.' The outline ruins of a mill can still be seen there just above the bridge.

The mill at Ponsworthy is known to have been sold in 1544 and operated until 1924. In its latter years it only ground meal for cattle, and the machinery was converted to drive a thresher and saw.

The mill also gave rise to a secondary industry, the bakery. Here bread, buns and cakes could be produced for the community. There are several examples of these 'sack ovens', to give them their correct title, on and around the moor. They are in themselves enlarged versions of the domestic bread oven.

## The Village Green and School

The village green at Widecombe is also the site for the village fair, first held on the 25 October 1850. Afterwards the organizers dined with the Reverend Holman Mason to celebrate its inauguration.

The old name for the village green at Widecombe was Buttes Park, the land set aside for archery practice. It was in the reign of Edward II 'that every Englishman should have a bow of his own height, of yew, ash, wych-hazel or amburn, and that butts should be made in every township'. The adjacent manors of Jordan and Spitchwick also had sites for this enterprise.

A study of the accounts of the great storm of 1638 show that on the site of the present green was a bowling-alley, kales or keels being the old name of this sport played by, among others, Sir Francis Drake.

Close to Dartmoor churches we find the church house, built originally for Parish festivities and church ales, in fact a brewhouse. Many have since become inns and public houses, some though like Widecombe have survived for the use of the parishioners.

The Widecombe church house, built about 1538, has been used as a school, poor house and alms house. When it first became a school is unknown, but Richard Hill, literatus, was licensed to teach in the parish in 1632. The upper floor provided the school room, children filing up the two stairways, boys on one side and girls on the other, while the Dame stood at the top. There are residents still living (1988) who attended school in the 1930s.

The first schools were charitable affairs and among their rules were that no child was to be admitted if their parents could pay. Children were to receive a maximum of three years schooling and when they left each was given a Bible and commanded to attend Sunday School.

The records show that the church house was considered to be capable of housing eight units when used as a poor house, one unit being the sexton's cottage. Visual proof of this can be found by counting the number of fireplaces.

Facing the church house is Glebe Farm, which stands on

land sold to the Church in 1283. Behind the Glebe is the vicarage, with the Parson's Barn between. Glebe Farm was part of the Vicar's income and he stored his tithes in its barn. The present vicarage is marked with signs of its many renovations, but cellars under the present building have been there for a very long time, with documentary evidence in 1684 and possibly 1613. An old beam found in the house inscribed HMB could relate to Hericus Magister Brusee, vicar in 1503–1532.

## The Smithy

The village artisan, so important to rural life, has now gone, but relics of his presence can still be seen in the buildings which housed his workshops and some of the tools and equipment of his trade.

Most villages had a blacksmith, and so it was with Widecombe and Ponsworthy. In both instances the forge still stands, the fires being extinguished for many years. In many cases the blacksmith assisted both the cordwainer, by fitting iron plates to shoes, and the wheelwright by fitting rims to wheels. The wheel-binding stone at Widecombe was broken up a few years ago but one still exists at Ponsworthy and other examples are found on the open moor.

Cecil Torr in *Small Talk at Wreyland* says 'I have seen an account set out between a blacksmith and a farmer without reference at all to money. On one side there were horseshoes, ploughshears, etc. and on the other side, pork, butter, geese, etc. And both parties reckoned the items up, and saw that the totals balanced. They seemed to have some weights and measures in their mind that are not found in books, say 4 horseshoes make 1 duck.'

ST PANCRAS CHURCH, WIDECOMBE
(sx 718 767)

The magnificent tower of Widecombe Church reaches 135ft towards the
sky. It is supported by buttresses built in three stages, topped by small
pinnacles. Larger crocketed octagonal pinnacles adorn the highest corners. It
was built at the turn of the sixteenth century.

WIDECOMBE CHURCH, INTERIOR

St Pancras is a typical cruciform church with nave, north and south aisles and transepts, chancel and north and south chantry aisles. The porch is on the south side and the vestry on the north-east corner. The cradle roof is supported on plain octagonal pillars with chamfered caps and bases. The back of the church is now empty but in 1815 the whole of the interior was filled with box pews designated by farms and individuals. The area in front of the tower was occupied by the singing loft where the choir and musicians sat.

CROSSES AND FONT, WIDECOMBE CHURCH

The three crosses standing at the side of the tower were found among
rubbish in the blocked off newel stairs; the old font was at one time built into
the stone wall that surrounds the churchyard.

GRAVESTONES

The interior of Widecombe Church contains few engraved tombstones,
though several hundred people were buried under the flagstones. Roger Hill
died in the great storm which struck the church in 1838. His friend Robert
Meade, the warrener, was buried next to him, the stone adorned with the
simple cross.

186

ALTAR STONE

The altar stone of the recently dedicated St Katherine's Chapel,
Widecombe, was for centuries buried in the floor, its authenticity is
confirmed by the five crosses engraved on its surface.

GRAFFITI, WIDECOMBE CHURCH

The lead roof of the tower was installed by the churchwardens in 1747. Since
then it has been subjected to graffiti, people scratching their names, initials
and dates.

## BOSSES

CHRIST

The medieval builder covered the joints of the roof beams with carved wooden bosses. At Widecombe they are also painted. It is to be regretted that due to years of deterioration various heads have been lost.

Symbols on bosses may be either Christian or pagan and some have several interpretations. The figurehead of Christ holding up his hands in blessing is self-explanatory; note that one thumb is missing.

ST KATHERINE

St Katherine was the patron saint of trades based on the wheel: millers,
spinners and wheelwrights. She holds a wheel in one hand and the martyrs
sword in the other.

GREEN MAN

There are several Green Men in Widecombe with foliage growing out of
their mouths and nostrils. 'Jack in the Green' was a pagan symbol carried
around on Mayday, celebrating the beginning of spring.

RABBITS

It is said the three rabbits or hares were an alchemist symbol for tin and this is a common motif in Dartmoor churches. It can be interpreted as the Trinity, and is also known as the 'Hunt of Venus'.

## STONE BOSSES

BEARDED MAN

WOMAN

CROWNED HEAD

There are five stone bosses at Widecombe, all on the windows of the chancel area. Three appear to be of the same bearded man as found on one of the roof bosses. One head has the smooth features of a woman, the other, above the window, appears to have a crown and may be the Virgin Mary.

WIDECOMBE CROSS

CROSS TREE

COFFIN STONE
(sx 677 733)

A broken cross was found and set up in the graveyard outside the south entrance. Its original base was in the square outside the Church House, now occupied by a yew tree, this tree is known as the Cross Tree.

The dead from the ancient tenements of Huccaby, Hexworthy, and those adjacent to the Dartmeet clapper bridge, were carried to Widecombe for burial. The bearers would rest on the Coffin Stone, a naturally cleft rock, as they climbed Yar Tor hill. The present road was cut much later. The two stones are adorned with crosses and initials.

## DARTMOOR GRAVESTONES

ANN HANNAFORD, WIDECOMBE
(sx 718 767)

Early gravestones are of granite, often engraved in the simplest manner.
Later, slate and other material became fashionable, and they were easier to
inscribe! Embossed granite stones would appear to be the oldest.

SW 1742, LYDFORD
(sx 509 847)

GRAVESTONES, MARY TAVY
(sx 509 787)

FRENCH OFFICER, MORETONHAMPSTEAD
(sx 755 861)

RKWBTLoDoM. 1616, SAMPFORD SPINEY
(sx 534 725)

A tomb in Sampford Spiney graveyard has initials and date, 1616, embossed on one side. It has stood the test of time very well. A stonemason, or the same workshop, cut simple and neat stones of a distinctive type which can be seen both in Lydford and Mary Tavy graveyards.

In Chagford graveyard is a small tomb with neat arched sides. Elsewhere a photograph of this stone described it improbably as a Roman altar. Many stones have inscriptions cut with little regard to the formation of the words; for example one at Widecombe.

In the parole towns around the moor can be found gravestones erected to French officers who died as prisoners of the Napoleonic War.

ROMAN ALTAR(?) CHAGFORD
(sx 702 875)

## WIDECOMBE, VILLAGE GREEN

Thousands of visitors walk on the Green at Widecombe. Its original name
was Buttes Park, the area set aside for archery practice. Here morris dancers
perform a ritual dance.

CHURCH HOUSE, WIDECOMBE

Church houses were originally used by the parishioners for festivities and church ales.

Widecombe Church house was used as a poor house, alms house and both as a charity and church school. Its first documentary evidence is dated 1608, though it was built about 1538, probably on the site of an older wooden house. It has a pentice (porch) on its south side, and on the north two sets of steps to the upper floor. Under these steps is the entrance to the ground floor. This arrangement can also be seen at the delightful church house of South Tawton, built about 1498.

CHURCH HOUSE, SOUTH TAWTON
(SX 653 945)

ALMSHOUSE, MORETONHAMPSTEAD
(sx 755 861)

This marvellous example of the rural mason's art was built, as the date over
the entrance states, in 1637. Its pentice is internal to the building. There
appears to have been a large window, or possibly a doorway to the upper
floor, now blocked up at the west end.

GLEBE FARM, WIDECOMBE

VICARAGE CELLARS

On the other side of the village square to the church house is Glebe Farm from which the vicar derived some of his income. At right angles to the Glebe on its south side is Parson's Barn where he kept some of his tithes. The vicarage stands only a few yards further south. This building shows on its outer surface the many changes and renovations it has been subject to.

Probably the only original part are its cellars which were built prior to the seventeenth century.

The Reverend Holman Mason was renowned for his port cellars, and it is likely he built the brick lining inside the original granite structure in the mid 1800s.

BLACKSMITH'S SHOP, PONSWORTHY
(sx 700 738)

ANVIL, WIDECOMBE

There has been a blacksmith's shop at Widecombe for centuries, regrettably it closed soon after the Second World War, though internal fittings survive.

TROUGH AND FORGE, WIDECOMBE

A crude granite trough was placed in front of the forge to quench the heated iron, which had been hammered and cut to shape on the anvil.

WHEEL-BINDING STONE, LYDFORD
(sx 509 847)

Wheel-binding stones are fairly common and were used by the blacksmith to put the iron rim onto wheels. The wheelwright would make the wheel and, aided by the blacksmith, it would be run up and down an iron strip to determine the length, and the ends of the strip flattened so that when bent into a circle and pinned together the thickness would remain even all round. The rim was then reheated and slipped over the wheel. Immediately it was doused with cold water to prevent burning, and the contraction on cooling bound the whole wheel together.

QUERN, PETER TAVY
(sx 517 778)

The rotary hand mill, or quern, was used by peasants for many centuries, while pounding grain in a mortar was still carried on in the Hebrides this century. There are many versions of this simple tool, one that Hansford Worth described as being almost complete at Sortridge is now at Peter Tavy. The rotating stone has a flat base, but some upper stones are grooved like mill stones. Another variant is the pot quern, this had no lip and the upper stone turned on a central wooden peg. In North Bovey church is a mortar in which grain was pounded into flour.

206

POT QUERN, HOLNE
(sx 706 695)

MORTAR, NORTH BOVEY
(sx 739 838)

MILLSTONES, PONSWORTHY
(sx 701 739)

Millstones are quite common on Dartmoor. The upper stones are grooved
to help the passage of the grains outwards as they rotate. The stones are
comparatively thin as can be seen in the photograph of Ponsworthy
millstones. The one found outside a barn at Babeny is probably a base stone,
and may never have been round.

MILLSTONE, BABENY
(sx 672 752)

PONSWORTHY MILL
(sx 701 739)

Ponsworthy settlement dates back until at least 1281, with the first recording of the mill in 1544 when it was sold to Richard Langworthy of Withecombe by the Earl of Bath. This mill was in use up until 1924, grinding meal, and in its later years, by the addition of wheels and belts, the water wheel was able to drive a saw and a thresher. The machinery has lain undisturbed since then.

BAKEHOUSE, PONSWORTHY
(sx 701 739)

In 1855/57 John Tollick the miller also described himself as a baker. The Bakehouse has been converted into a private residence. The industrial sack oven produced bread and rolls, possibly cakes, for the local population. It was an enlarged version of the household bread oven, used in exactly the same way, being heated by burning half-a-dozen faggots (bundles of sticks) and furze (gorse).

BAKEHOUSE OVEN, PONSWORTHY

# 9
# TRACKWAYS
# AND ROADS

Ancient trackways abound on Dartmoor. When, how or why they were built, we may only guess, but the many well-worn footpaths that the walker comes across, are often no more than animal tracks. This would have been the case when man first ventured upon these moorlands. With the coming of the herdsman the narrow path became a track as he drove his beasts before him. From these humble beginnings developed the roads and trackways that can be seen on the moor today.

There is no direct evidence of trackways joining the many prehistoric settlements scattered over the moor, even though mention has already been made of the short droveways found on some sites. In historic times, the meandering lane or path circumnavigated land boundaries, giving access to remote farms, proceeding from village to farming hamlet, to profitable mine workings, or to peat workers' habitat.

Religious houses had a major effect on travel and trade. The oldest was the Benedictine monastery at Tavistock, dedicated to St Mary and St Rumon, founded, it is believed by Ordgar, Earl of Devon in 961, and completed by his son Ordolf. It did not have a very auspicious beginning, for the Anglo Saxon Chronicle records 997 as the date of its destruction by the Danes who 'burned Ordolf's Minster of Tavistock, and brought unspeakable booty with them to their ships.' It was rebuilt and survived for another five hundred years.

The Benedictine Abbey of Buckfast, on the opposite side of the moor, was founded by Earl Aylward in 1018, one of its great benefactors being King Cnut. St Mary's Abbey also fell on hard times but was revitalised by the Cistercian monks from Savigny in 1136. The present Abbey has been rebuilt along the outline of the original foundations.

Buckland Abbey, a few miles south of Tavistock, owed its foundation to two great ladies, Amicia, Countess of Devon, Lady of the Isle, and her daughter, Isabella de Fortibus. Amicia invited the Cistercian monks of Quarr Abbey in the Isle of Wight to colonize Buckland, and they were firmly established by 1280. Among its thousands of acres were gifts by Isabella, which included the Manor of Walkhampton.

All three Abbeys ended their days with the dissolution during Henry VIII's reign.

A growing trade between these great houses saw routes being established. In addition, the monks would want to carry out their pastoral duties, and this would greatly influence the siting of the actual path. Crosses were set up marking such routes.

The first road makers proper in Britain were the Romans, but there is no evidence that they penetrated the upland moor. After the Romans left no real attempt was made to build roads until the eighteenth and nineteenth centuries, and previous to this there only existed packhorse tracks. Polwhele says of these animals that they 'are admirably well adapted ... very hardy ... endure great fatigue. They carry heavy burthens up and down precipices with a wonderful agility.' Of their tracks John Vowell says of those who 'travelled in this countrie but one Journey they can forebeare the second'.

An Act of Parliament passed in 1696 gave Justices the power to erect at crossroads guidestones bearing letters indicating the next town, though the marking of trackways with direction signs goes back a great many years before it became a statutory requirement.

When Benjamin Donn in 1765 produced his large scale, one inch to the mile, map of Devon, he recorded tracks that crossed the central divide of Dartmoor. One went from 'Merriville Bridge' over Long Ash Common to Hexworthy, Holne and Ashburton. The track is marked by set stones, mostly untrimmed, bearing the letters A for Ashburton and T for Tavistock. Many of these stones have been taken and used as gateposts. There is no doubt that a survey of Dartmoor gateposts should uncover a number of exciting finds. It is also interesting to note that the stones indicated on Donn's map match the known sightings.

When the traveller came to the banks of the numerous streams and rivers which barred the way, they had to be crossed either by wading, or presumably jumping from rock to rock until gaining the other side. The rider would have to find a convenient fording place.

The moving of rocks into position near a fording place to form stepping stones and the development of the track by constant use to that fording place naturally followed. But we know the people of Babeny and Pizwell in 1260 found it eight miles to Lydford in good weather and fifteen miles in foul. The answer was to erect a bridge, known locally as a clapper. In its basic form it is a single large slab well supported at each end. This common form can be found all over the moor, not just crossing streams but leats as well; and in this latter case one often finds bridges without water to cross.

Where the main packhorse trade routes required a more substantial clapper bridge, one with several slabs being supported on piers was built well clear of the water. An earth and stone embankment was required on both sides.

The clapper bridge dates from 1400, possibly earlier. It was unsuitable for wheeled traffic; bridges being more suitable for the carriage and wain came into being in the nineteenth century.

It is often difficult to date the building of a bridge, for not until an Act of 1888 did it become a duty of a public body to construct bridges. Up until this time religious zeal, private benevolence and enlightened self-interest are the likely causes, but once built it became part of the highway and therefore came under the jurisdiction of the waywardens. Though some bridges cannot be dated, many have stones in their parapets giving dates of repairs.

There were two types of bridge, those known as County Bridges (these were the responsibility of the Justices of the Peace who appointed their own surveyor), and 'local' bridges. Apart from the solid structure of the bridge the County maintained three hundred feet of the highway on either side, the point being denoted by a set stone engraved with the letter C.

The waywarden was responsible for the local bridge, and the accounts for Widecombe show that any crossing of a stream was so titled, even the flow of water in a covered channel was termed a bridge.

In 1823 it was required by law that those responsible for roads 'shall cause stones or posts to be set up or placed in or near the sides of every Turnpike Road, at the distance of One mile from each other' – and what a lovely variety of milestones can be found on and around Dartmoor. The Turnpike, a stretch of road sponsored under an Act of Parliament, was the remedy to the past ills of lack of maintenance.

The Okehampton Trust was started in 1760 followed two years later by the Tavistock Trust. The limit of the Trust was marked by a suitably engraved stone, as were specific instructions to users, and special events, like that outside Kelly College which states 'THIS ROAD WAS MADE BY PUBLIC SUBSCRIPTION IN A PERIOD OF GREAT DISTRESS 1817'.

For those interested in studying the development of

our road system the author recommends a study of the road which now crosses the moor from Tavistock to Moretonhampstead. On this route can be seen the development from packhorse track, through the 1772 Turnpike Trusts of Tavistock and Moretonhampstead, to present day modernisation. It has along its length medieval crosses, direction stones and a variety of milestones. At Postbridge can be seen a ford, stepping stones, clapper bridge and Turnpike bridge – this has been modernised with long ramps, because the motorist hated to bang the top of his head going over its humpback – and at Merrivale a modern bridge has been laid over the old ford to ease the motorist's way.

215

FERNWORTHY
(sx 663 839)

It is only in times of drought that the early medieval clapper bridge and late
medieval bridge built for packhorses and wains can be seen. They are now
submerged below the waters of Fernworthy reservoir.

HAWSON'S CROSS
(sx 711 682)

TWO THORNS BASE
(sx 678 707)

No name has been given to a track which goes from Buckfast Abbey across the moor to either Tavistock or Buckland Abbey, though it is marked by a line of crosses. Its route was via Hockmoor, Hawson's Cross, Play Cross, to Holne Moor Gate, to Horns Cross. There is a possible cross base according to Andrew Fleming just west of the southern end of Venford Reservoir, neatly positioned at the head of a disused stroll named by Fleming 'Two Thorns Cross'. To give more substance to this claim Crossing believed a cross once stood near Workman's Ford which is close by. From Horns the track crossed the O Brook by way of Horse Ford Cross, onto Down Ridge, to Skaur Ford. Far away on the horizon can be seen the first of two crosses

on the summit of Ter Hill. The route continued down to Mount Misery, past Childe's Tomb of the gory legend which has an historical basis, Goldsmith's and Nuns Cross. From here the track swung round the head of Newleycombelake and descends to Riddipit Steps, now Leather Tor Bridge, by way of a modern cross set in an old base stone. It then continued to Newleycombelake Cross, and Crazywell Cross. Beyond the bridge the trackway passed Crossgate and Lower Lowery Cross (now missing), to Yannadon Cross (now returned). From here the track could go direct to Buckland or just as easily could lead below Whitchurch Down to Tavistock.

HORNS CROSS
(sx 669 711)

HORSE FORD CROSS
(sx 660 714)

SKAUR FORD CROSS
(sx 655 715)

TER HILL CROSSES (looking east)
(sx 642 707)

MOUNT MISERY
(sx 637 706)

Mount Misery Cross on the west flank of Ter Hill, named it is said from the work involved in clearing the land hereabouts. From this position it is possible to see the way round Fox Tor Mire and the next three crosses: Childe's Tomb, Goldsmith's and Nuns Cross, the latter is obscured by the modern building almost against the horizon.

CHILDE'S TOMB
(sx 624 702)

GOLDSMITH'S CROSS
(sx 616 702)

NUNS CROSS
(sx 605 699)

CROSSGATE
(sx 562 695)

Nuns Cross or more correctly Siward's Cross has the name SIWARD engraved on one side and BOC LOND on the other, both below incised crosses. When Amicia granted lands to Buckland Abbey 'Syward cross' is named as a bound, so BOC LOND was added after the time 'Crucem Sywardi' was named in the 1240 perambulation.

Crossing and Hoskins say the Siward, Earl of Northumberland, held the Manors of Tavei (Mary Tavy) and Wifleurde (Willsworthy) during Edward the Confessor's reign. Holinshed says in his *Histoire of England* (for 1054),

that 'Siward the noble earle of Northumberland with a great power of horsseman went into Scotland and in battel put to flight Mackbeth, that had vsurped the crowne of Scotland, and that done, placed Malcomle surnamed Camoir, the sonne of Duncanne, some time King of Scotland, in government of that realme.'

These are some of the characters we have become acquainted with from reading Shakespeare's *Macbeth*, Siward, being of such stature, has his name commemorated on this cross.

## TAVISTOCK/ASHBURTON TRACK STONES

SOUTH FLANK NORTH HESSARY TOR
(sx 640 726)

The Track marked by Donn from Merrivale Bridge to Hexworthy, then by way of Combestone Tor, Holne Moor Gate, Holne Bridge to Ashburton, was marked between the first two places by moorstone posts engraved with the letters T for Tavistock and A for Ashburton. The letter facing towards the traveller, denotes the town they have come from. A number of these are photographed where they had fallen, but recently they have been re-erected. One, near the Merrivale/Long Ash car park, formerly used as a gatepost, has recently been moved a few yards and set up in the wall. Close by on the ground was found another stone cut with the single letter T, and this has been set up above the original gateway.

MERRIVALE
(sx 554 751)

LONG ASH COMMON
(sx 558 746)

SWINCOMBE
(sx 573 738)

## DIRECTION STONES

STINIEL
(sx 701 852)

STONY POST
(sx 717 703)

Direction stones abound on the moor. These photographs show a selection of stones showing the letter A for Ashburton. There is an interesting feature with the A having a bar across the top **Ā** or a V cross bar **Λ**, this also appears on the SABINI FILI MACCODECHETI stone. Typographic experts think it is just a local interpretation of that letter, though it is thought-provoking that it originated by A.D. 550.

The CHAGF/ORD splitting of the word is very common and other examples will be found elsewhere in this book.

The only dated stone recorded here is at Stone Cross above Cockingford, inscribed 1790 over NEW/TON, W for Widecombe and on its other side ASH/BUR/TON.

CROSS FURZES
(sx 699 669)

MOORCROSS
(sx 704 640)

CHAGF/ORD
(sx 688 827)

STONE CROSS, COCKINGFORD
(sx 719 745)

STEPPING STONES, LAUGHTER HOLE
(sx 663 757)

Along the track of many an ancient Dartmoor route, stones were levered into position to form stepping stones to ease the way across rivers and streams. The author's children loved to play 'first across' as depicted in the photograph, three of them leaping over the stepping stones of Laughter Hole.

STEPPING STONES, POSTBRIDGE
(sx 647 789)

CLAPPER BRIDGE, WALLABROOK (TEIGN)
(sx 653 872)

The basic clapper bridge was the single large slab laid from bank to bank, the edge of the stream often reinforced with stones. This single-span specimen is at 'Wotesbrokelakesfote' of the 1240 perambulation. It has certainly not been in place since that time, for just downstream the Teign-ever Clapper was washed away and three cut stones, strapped together by iron, replaced the original clapper.

CLAPPER BRIDGE, POSTBRIDGE
(sx 647 789)

CLAPPER BRIDGE, TEIGNHEAD FARM
(sx 639 845)

This multi-span clapper of untrimmed stones was still being built in 1790 when Teignhead Farm was being won from the open moor. That these dry stone bridges have withstood the onslaught of storm waters is a tribute to the builders; others are known to have been washed away and rebuilt. The clapper at Bellever, depicted after a winter thaw, shows the waters near the top of the piers. This clapper was in use in 1809 and it is likely that the missing stones were removed after the road bridge was built nearby.

BELLEVER BRIDGES
(sx 658 774)

BEETOR CROSS
(sx 714 842)

The route of the two Turnpike Trust roads from Tavistock to Moretonhampstead were probably marked with crosses for centuries before the Turnpike Acts were passed. At least one other cross, as well as the seven that now remain, has been recorded.

Beetor Cross at the Watching Place was found close to its present position and re-erected. Leapra Cross stands at the junction of this ancient packhorse track and the Mariners Way. Bennett's Cross, the origin of its name open to speculation, is a long established marker, being used as a parish bound, a Birch Tor Vitifer mine bound, and as a bound for Headland Warren. It is inscribed with the letters W.B. (see Introduction).

LEAPRA CROSS
(sx 702 834)

The Reverend Bray recorded a cross above Merripit at the turn of the nineteenth century. It was then fallen and has since disappeared. He recorded a further cross at Postbridge, but all that can now be found is part of the head built into a wall.

The Windy Post stands on the old route from Merrivale, across Beckamoor Coombe to Moortown, thence across Whitchurch Down, past Pixies Cross and another much battered), before the track reached Tavistock.

POSTBRIDGE
(sx 652 792)

WINDY POST
(sx 533 743)

PIXIES CROSS
(sx 502 730)

WHITCHURCH DOWN
(sx 493 738)

COUNTY STONE, PONSWORTHY
(sx 702 741)

TURNPIKE TRUST
(sx 527 859)

That part of the highway either side of a bridge whose upkeep was the responsibility of the Justices of the Peace, was defined by a stone engraved with the letter C, being placed three hundred feet either side of the bridge. Many of these stones have disappeared.

The termination of many of the routes of the Okehampton Turnpike Trust are marked with stones stating END OF / OKEHAMPTON / TRUST. This one stands close to a Lydford-Bridestowe Parish bound.

Trusts were able to stipulate the number of horses allowed by wagoners on a particular stretch of road, in order to avoid undue damage. On steep inclines extra horses were allowed. Standing close to the Beardon Take Off

Stone there are two round stones with metal fitments for tethering the extra horse that under the terms of the Trust had to be taken off at this point. Dave Brewer records that there are two or three more take off stones, one in Lydford and one at Hurdwick, acting as gateposts.

We do not know when many of Dartmoor's bridges were originally built, but those who repaired them recorded the fact by stating so on an engraved stone (or just the date). The words cut on Drakeford Bridge outside Lustleigh state: THIS 1684/BRIDG WAS/REPARED/BY THE/COUNTY.

TAKE OFF, BEARDON
(sx 518 842)

DRAKEFORD BRIDGE, LUSTLEIGH
(sx 789 802)

## MILESTONES

13 MILES TO PLYMº
(sx 515 739)

Milestones also appear in their own intriguing variations. The old Peter Tavy-Plymouth track has, at Pennycomequick, its thirteen mile marker with the letters cut diagonally, the fourteenth marker's letters are cut horizontally. They have a twin in the fourteen mile stone on another old track from Tavistock which joins the other a few hundred yards above the Pennycomequick stone.

Parole Towns for Napoleonic prisoners also have mile markers measured from the edge of town, denoting the limits of free movement for parolees. The Druidshill marker says simply '1 Mile'.

14 MILES TO PLYM°
(sx 492 740)

PAROLE BOUND, DRUIDSHILL
(sx 748 713)

TAVISTOCK TURNPIKE, TWO BRIDGES
(sx 608 749)

A milestone on the old bridge at Two Bridges is one of a variety on this road. The Moretonhampstead Turnpike set up their mile stones all engraved (X) MILES/FROM/MORETON. They start from the edge of town, it being a Parole town. All the figures are of the same figuration except 4 which is cut with IIII vertical lines. At the other end, outside Tavistock, the 19th milestone also gives the distance to Truro.

MORETONHAMPSTEAD TURNPIKE
(sx 700 834)

TAVISTOCK TURNPIKE
(sx 500 746)

WIDECOMBE/NATSWORTHY
(sx 723 781)

One mile from Widecombe on the Natsworthy road is a lovely example (on a parole stone?) of local pronunciation, while outside Lydford Castle is the simplistic configuration of eight miles to Tavistock and nine to Okehampton. Among the greatest distances recorded must be that on a stone in Tavistock which records London as being 215 miles away!

LYDFORD CASTLE
(sx 509 847)

TAVISTOCK TOWN
(sx 482 745)

TOLLHOUSE
(sx 494 747)

The cost of keeping the turnpike in a reasonable state of repair was met by levying tolls at various points. On the Tavistock-Moretonhampstead road toll gates were established at Rundlestone, Postbridge, Moorgate and Bughead. The only tollhouse remaining on this route stands one mile east of Tavistock, easily identifiable by its distinctive windows set at angles so that the toll collector could watch for travellers.

# 10
# THE TIN
# INDUSTRY

The earliest references to tin working on Dartmoor are from the middle of the twelfth century, and great speculation is made of its lack of record in the Domesday Book. Tin extraction is without doubt the most extensive industrial activity ever undertaken on Dartmoor, and has the greatest impact on the landscape.

William de Wrotham, 1198, was commanded to look into the 'just weights of tin' and in his report he says, 'All the diggers and buyers of black tin, and the first smelters of tin, and traders in tin of the first smelting, shall have the just and ancient customs and liberties established in Devonshire and Cornwall'. It was therefore an old and well established industry by then and this is confirmed by King John in 1201 who granted a charter confirming the rights of the tinners based on ancient custom.

Charters issued by Edward I in 1305 separated the tinners of Cornwall and Devon and established in Devon the Stannaries: Ashburton, Tavistock and Chagford, later Plympton also became a Stannary Court, all under the leadership of a warden. Twenty-four jurors, elected by the tinners from each stannary, held a Great Parliament at Crocken Tor. Those who broke the stannary laws were imprisoned at Lydford.

Among the rights granted and reaffirmed by Edward I was the statement 'We have also granted to the same tin miners that they may be enabled to dig tin and turves for casting tin everywhere in our lands, moors and wastes and those of all others whatsoever in the county aforesaid; and to divert streams and water-courses for the workings of the stannaries aforesaid where and as often as there shall be need; and to buy firewood for the casting of tin, as was the custom of old, without hinderance from us or our heirs, from Bishops, Abbots, Priors, Earls, Barons, or any others whatsoever.'

This gave the tinner unprecedented power which in the end was to prove his undoing. Richard Strode, a tinner, or adventurer in tin works, was also Member of Parliament for Plympton in 1512. Strode introduced an Act in Parliament which would have curtailed the tinners' ancient rights. However, because Strode was a tinner, himself, his fellow tinners fined him in each of the Stannary Courts and eventually imprisoned him at Lydford. Fortunately a writ from the Exchequer released him after three weeks.

Strode put all his grievances into an Act of Parliament which went on to lay down the right of freedom of speech that all M.P.s enjoy today. The Act also established the more important point that a lower court does not have jurisdiction over a higher one.

The Stannary Courts were abolished in 1836, the last being held it is believed in 1786.

The tinner, and we can assume would-be tinner, had only to mark his claim. This was quite simple according to Pryce. 'They are limited by holes cut in the turf, and the soil turned back upon the turf which is cut, in the form of a mole hill'.

Four bounds, straight lines between each, defined the claim which was renewed annually. Three rocks leaning against each other were also acceptable as bounds, and letters cut on a set stone established a more permanent site.

The tinner categorized three types of tin ore: stream, shode and bal (or mine) tin. The latter was the ore as it was to be found in lodes or veins. Erosion of these lodes, mainly by streams cutting through them, produced first the shode and then the stream tin.

Shode according to Pryce 'is pebbly, or smoothly angular, of various sizes, from half an ounce to some pounds weight' and it lay nearest to the lode. Stream tin comprised fine sands that were washed further downstream to be spread out over the valley floor.

The first 'tinners' would have found tin in a very pure state cast up on the riverbanks at almost every meander. The next step was to turn over the valley bottoms where deposits of very high quality tin sands would be found. This is often referred to as streaming for tin, which is not really correct, for streaming actually refers to using water as a means of uncovering the ore.

Two distinct types of working can be seen in the valley bottoms: first haphazard digging and piling of up the refuse, which can be seen in the valley of the Glazebrook and in the upper reaches of the Meavy. Then came a very systematic method where the tinner would build a wall of large stones, throwing the remaining earth and rubble over the wall as he uncovered the strata of tin below. Excellent examples of such 'burrows' are seen in the valley of the Erme and its tributary the Blacklane Brook. The tinner may have diverted water along the face of the wall to help clear the refuse. This type of working can also be seen in the upper reaches of Beckamoor Coombe, just above the Tavistock-Princetown road.

Tin streaming was described by an anonymous tinner in 1671, thus: 'Then we go to the sides of those Hills most suspected to have any loads in them, where there may be a conveniency of bringing a little stream of water (the more the better), and cut a Leat, Gurt, or Trench, about 2 foot over, and as deep as the Shelf (bedrock granite), in which we turn the water to run 2 or 3 dayes: by which time the water, by washing away the filth from the stones, and looser parts of the earth, will easily discover, what Shoad is there.'

Once the 'tin-stuff' was reclaimed from the ground it had to be refined, or smelted, and cast into blocks. The black tinner had done his job and the white tinner, who did the smelting, took over. In 1290 there were 473 black tinners and 302 white, but by 1300 records show 440 black tinners, with their white compatriots fallen to 93. This could be seen as evidence that Jews, expelled in 1291, worked in the blowing houses, known locally as Jew's Houses.

The earliest mention of tin smelting is thought to occur in the 1240 perambulation, one of the bounds being Furnum Regis, recorded as Kinge's Oven in 1608, and as Kings Oven on O.S. maps.

Blowing houses are marked in several places on O.S. maps, always close to streams. Most of these sites date from between the fifteenth to the seventeenth century. It was here that tin was processed. A leat brought water to power the wheel which drove 'stamps' and leather bellows that supplied a continuous blast of air to the furnace.

The fuel was peat, of this John Vowell says: 'They do digge in sundrye meete and convenyent places great turffes wch beinge dryed is a verye good fuel and is spent in blowenge of their tynne and other fuell they have not.'

In front of the furnace was the float, a channelled block of granite into which the molten tin would run. From there it would be transferred to the mould. Mould stones were usually near the door, and many have small test moulds cut into the top edge.

There may be as many as a hundred blowing house sites still to be seen on the moor, plus a great many other buildings of similar age used, it is believed, by the tinners.

Before tin-stone (ore) was smelted it was broken down to convenient size by hammering, mechanical stamp, or ground in a mill. In some cases the breaking down process was carried out on the same site, even in the same building as the furnace. Other sites seem to indicate a separate building for this purpose, and that when broken down and dried, according to Pryce, it was easier to transport to a more distant blowing house.

The mortar stone forms the base of the stamping mill where Carew says there are: 'three, and in some places six great logs of timber, bound at the ends with iron, and lifted up and down by a wheel driven with water.' He continues, 'From the stamping mill it passeth to the crazing-mill, which bruiseth the same to a fine sand, Howbeit, of late times they mostly use wet stampers, and so have no need of the crazing-mills for their best stuff, but only for the crust of their tails.'

The evidence from mortar stones would indicate on Dartmoor that at each site there were either two or three stamps. There is still one excellent example of a crazing-mill on the moor. This device ground the larger tin gravel into fine sand, after the tin had been separated from all the non-metallic residues in settling pits or buddles.

There are two further types of distinctive tinners' building. One is the 'barracks', a small building with a raised bench for sleeping on, for one or two tinners, or sometimes a larger building for the team workers when staying on site. There is also a 'cache' which from its size was used as a storeroom. When the alluvial deposits had been worked out, the tinner had to dig down to the lode; this led inevitably to the tinner working deep underground.

There does not seem to be much evidence for mining before the turn of the eighteenth century, although the conical depression formed at the top of a shaft can be found in many gerts, the deep open-cast workings.

Mines suffered from water seepage and those above the valley bottom were drained by horizontal tunnels, or adits. In later mines the adit could also provide an entrance. Adits and shafts are not uncommon on the moor and they are dangerous and should not be entered. The author can well remember one dry spring morning standing by a shaft of the Golden Dagger mine and listening to the sound of a 'Niagara' falling somewhere far below.

At least three closed adits can be found on the Birch Tor Vitifer mine complex by evidence of the heavy flow of water from their sealed entrances.

De-watering of a mine was done either by using a water wheel to generate power to raise and lower buckets, or by a whim which Pryce defined as 'a horse engine'. The whim itself was a cylinder to which pulleys with a long rope were attached. A barrel was tied to each end of the rope which turned round the cylinder, one empty barrel descending while a full one rose to the surface. Traces of the whim-round and granite footsteps are found on the Eylesbarrow complex. The same systems raised the ore and the 'deads', all the waste material, from the shafts and levels.

Once the ore was brought to the surface and stamped to a fine sand, the tin was separated from the unwanted residues in buddles. Round buddles are common in the later mines, while at Eylesbarrow earlier rectangular pits can be seen adjacent to the line of stamping houses.

At the nineteenth century Eylesbarrow mine, the smelting house is now very ruined. It measures about sixty feet by twenty feet and appears to have two furnaces, one of the blast or blowing type, the other of the reverberating kind. It is the only mine smelting house on the Moor, it then being usual to take the ore off the moor for refining into tin.

The blast furnace at Eylesbarrow can be determined by the six massive blocks which formed its sides, three of which are still in position. From the furnace a flue seventy-four feet in length led to a chimney, now fallen. The flue has baffles along its length to prevent any tin escaping into the air.

Finally, two descriptions of the tinner who changed so much of Dartmoor's landscape: John Vowell says, 'The one is called the spader the daylie worker or laborer in the tynn-workes, and theire is no laborer to be compared unto him: for his apparell is course, his dyet sklender, his lodgings hard, his feedynge commonly course breade and hard cheese, and his drincke is water, and for lacke of a cuppe he drynketh it out of his spade or shovell: and he goeth so nere the weather as no man can lyve more frugally and nerer than he dothe. His lyffe most commonly is in pyttes and caves under grounde of a greate depth and in greate daunger because the earthe above his hedd is in sundry places crossed and posted over with tymber, to keepe the same from fallinge.'

Carew continues the characterisation, 'I have already told you how great charge the tinner undergoeth before he can bring his ore to this last mill, whereto if you add his care and cost in buying the wood for this service, in felling, framing and piling it to be burned, in fetching the same when it is cooled, through such far, foul, and cumbersome ways to the blowing-house, together with the blowers "two or three months" extreme and increasing labour, sweltering heat, danger of scalding their bodies, burning the houses, casting away the work, and lastly their ugly countenances tanned with smoke and besmeared with sweat: all these things (I say) being duly considered, I know not whether you would more marvel either whence a sufficient gain should arise to countervail so manifold expenses, or that gain could train men to undertake such pains and peril. But there let us leave them, since their own will doth bring them thither.'

MORTAR STONE, SOUSSONS
(sx 672 796)

The distinctive mortar stone formed the base of the stamp for crushing the
tin ore. When a stone base became worn it was moved or turned over, as in
the case of the Soussons stone, which has been re-used, twice on one side
and once on the other.

ERME BURROWS

The tinner dug short trenches, piling large stones up to form a wall and throwing the refuse over the top. He frequently used water to wash away earth and rock. In the valley of the Erme these burrows seem to indicate an organized procedure of advancement up the valley bottom following the course of the stream.

250

RESERVOIR, HAMELDOWN
(sx 710 786)

RESERVOIR HATCH, SHAPLEY TOR
(sx 698 823)

The tinner, assessing a likely spot, would build a reservoir, leading water to it along a leat. When ready he would open the hatch and allow the water to pour down the line of the suspected ore, washing away the soil and exposing the precious metal below. This was termed streaming for tin.

In wet weather the reservoir at the head of a gert near Stoneslade Tor, Hameldown still fills with water. Just north of Shapley Tor the tinners built a crescent shaped wall to hold back water, with a granite hatch for releasing the impounded flood.

## BLOWING HOUSES

**BLACKSMITH'S SHOP, TEIGNHEAD FARM**
(sx 638 843)

The name Blacksmith's Shop is given to the blowing house near Teignhead Farm. Part of its outline is quite distinct and its main features are a large upright granite block which may have been a part of the furnace known as the castle. Close by is a large double mould, another double but broken mould rests on top of a wall near the river.

BLOWING HOUSE, MERRIVALE BRIDGE
(sx 553 753)

The blowing house just above Merrivale Bridge has the best example of a furnace on the moor. Its shape is easily distinguishable and it has its float, though disturbed, in front of the furnace. A fine mould lies beside the door.

BLOWING HOUSES, BLACK TOR FALLS
(sx 575 716)

There are two tinners' buildings at Black Tor Falls, one on each side of the river. The number XIII is cut into the large door lintel of the left bank building, which appears to have contained a furnace. The right bank building had a very substantial fireplace and chimney, now destroyed. No one has recorded moulds in either house. There are a number of mortar stones, but as they are frequently moved it is difficult to say to which house they originally belonged.

BLOWING HOUSE, THE BOILER, SWINCOMBE
(sx 625 712)

There are at least three examples of what can be described as twin buildings on Dartmoor: Black Tor Falls, Week Ford, and at the Boiler (the point where the Swincombe River leaves Fox Tor Mire). Here the two buildings use a common leat, both have substantial fireplaces but neither appear to have either moulds or mortars. The environs of Fox Tor Mire saw tinners at their labours for many centuries. The lower house depicted here has a stone inside the doorway with H C 1753 shallowly cut on its surface.

## MORTAR STONES

DATED STONE, SWINCOMBE
(SX 625 712)

MORTAR STONE, BLACK TOR FALLS
(SX 575 712)

MORTAR STONE, RIDDIPIT
(SX 571 703)

MORTAR STONE, GOBBET
(SX 645 727)

The regularity of the pits formed by continuous stamping indicate that on Dartmoor two and three stamp heads was the usual practice. Mortar stones varied in size from large boulders to quite small pieces. They were often re-used, either by moving them sideways or by turning the stone over.

MORTAR STONE, WEEK FORD
(sx 662 724)

MORTAR STONE, WEEK FORD

## MOULDS

TEIGNHEAD FARM
(sx 638 843)

TEIGNHEAD FARM (broken mould)

The molten tin flowed from the furnace out into the float from whence it was transferred to the mould. Moulds vary in size and thus the weight of ingots varies, usually between 100 and 200 pounds. The mould's sides were bevelled to allow the ingot to be removed with ease. A small test mould, sometimes a shallow depression, sometimes a small hole, is often to be seen on the edge of the mould stone. The majority of moulds are singles but doubles are numerous enough not to be considered rarities.

The more pebbly tin sand was ground fine in a crazing mill, not unlike the action of the medieval grist mill. The only example of an upper and lower stone is to be seen at Gobbet in the Swincombe Valley. Baring-Gould says the upper stone is grooved but it is too heavy to check. The four holes in its upper surface were the attachment points for a turning mechanism, probably a lever moved by the tinner. There is no sign of a whim plat to indicate a horse was used.

WEEK FORD
(sx 662 724)

CRAZING MILL, GOBBET — UPPER STONE
(sx 645 727)

GOBBET
(sx 645 727)

CRAZING MILL, GOBBET — LOWER STONE

## CACHES

BEEHIVE HUT, EAST DART
(sx 639 814)

DOWNING'S HOUSE, ERME
(sx 639 629)

The tinner, having made his way to his tinworks, made a small shelter for his tools and possibly for himself. This shelter, referred to as a cache, varies in style, one marked on the O.S. Map above Postbridge as 'Beehive Hut' is a low structure with the walls being sloped inwards. A more complete version is found on the banks of the Erme, known locally as Downing's House.

A common cache construction was to under-dig a large boulder and build up sides and front wall. Another type was made by digging a tunnel into the growan and then hollowing out an enlarged chamber inside.

The Ordnance Survey have marked one at Leather Tor Farm as *fogou*, the Cornish word for a hidden chamber. This appears as a dark patch in a green bank on the outside, but has been built up and lined with stones on the inside.

COMBSHEAD
(sx 589 685)

FOGOU, LEATHER TOR FARM
(sx 567 697)

STONE TOR BOTTOM
(sx 647 858)

FOGOU (INTERIOR)

VITIFER MINE 'DRY'
(sx 682 809)

This view of the Vitifer 'dry' in 1948 was the first picture taken by the
author. Now there is only an outline on the ground and but a single wall of
the building remains. Crossing the valley to Chaw Gully the author then
photographed the bomb crater, all that remained of the engine house.
The engine house of the Wheal Betsy Mine is the only one on Dartmoor
with its chimney still intact.

BOMB CRATER
(sx 686 807)

ENGINE HOUSE, WHEAL BETSY
(sx 510 814)

ADIT
(sx 687 807)

The adit was originally a de-watering channel but in later mines was used as the entrance. This example of a short length driven under the Round Pound at Batworthy illustrates the amount of water covering the floor and how difficult it must have been to cut a tunnel through the heart of Dartmoor.

The shaft in Chaw Gully has in the author's lifetime always been highly dangerous. Only a few broken wires protected the unwary from falling in and it came as a relief to see it filled in a few years ago. Note the wood shuttering, the durns, which once prevented the loose earth of the cone from falling into the shaft. The author has dropped many a stone in his youth to hear it rebounding off the walls to end in a splash far below.

The area or sett of both tin works and mines were bounded by some form of marker. The Staple Tor sett has two bounds on the line of what must have been a very recognizable feature, the old packhorse track from Merrivale to Moortown. Here the letters SB are cut on a natural boulder, and on the far side of Beckamoor Coombe, not far from the Windy Post, is a set stone also marked SB. It is interesting to note the northern limit of this sett would appear to be the same line as the Pu Tor granite sett.

The later miners of the two mines, Birch Tor/Vitifer mine and the East Birch Tor mine, sometimes erroneously called the Headland mine, attacked the lode from both sides of the hill. A bound stone setting the limit of the East Birch Tor mine stands on the floor of Chaw Gully near the end of the triple stone row.

The original tinner's bound was three turves, often three stones propped against each other. The example shown may be just a natural feature, but it lies on grassy land above the Walkham not far from the right bank blowing house above Shillapark.

SHAFT
(sx 663 868)

EAST BIRCH TOR BOUND
(sx 689 809)

STAPLE BOUND
(sx 541 748)

TINNER'S BOUND(?)
(sx 765 551)

SMELTING HOUSE, EYLESBARROW
(sx 592 676)

The Eylesbarrow complex has many interesting features of early mining activity. The smelting house, once recorded as a blowing house, has decayed a great deal since Burnard photographed its walls. The chimney at the end of the long flue, which has partially collapsed since the author first saw it, has fallen. It had two furnaces, a blast or blowing furnace now seen as six large blocks, three fallen, with the flue above, and a reverberatory furnace. This is also made of large cut stones to be seen amongst the rubble of the former walls towards the near end of the building.

FLUE

STAMPING HOUSE, EYLESBARROW
(sx 595 680)

STAMPING HOUSE

There were several stamping houses at Eylesbarrow, now mainly seen as wheel pits with large trimmed blocks adjacent. It was to these blocks that the axle of the stamps connected. One stamping house wall still stands with the axle bearing, looking like a hole, still in position.

Two flat rod systems for transferring power from waterwheels to shafts can be viewed by the lines of stones set in pairs, each with its bearing mark.

The stone lined tunnel shown in the photograph extends from the exterior of one shaft. Perhaps water raised from the shaft might have flowed clear along its length.

A whim plat, a circular area with a granite footstep in its centre, can be seen at the northern end of the Eylesbarrow complex, not far from the track to Nuns Cross.

FLAT ROD BEARING STONE

FLAT ROD SYSTEM
(sx 599 683)

TUNNEL

WHIM STONE
(sx 601 684)

BUDDLE, RECTANGULAR, EYLESBARROW
(sx 595 680)

The buddle or settling pit was where the material from the stamps was washed and sorted. The heavy tin sand sank to the bottom and the refuse floated away. By continual stirring, the fine high quality tin ore was deposited first, with larger pebbles being cast further out, so that it was only the 'tails' that required to be ground further down in the crazing mill.

Buddles at Eylesbarrow are rectangular, the earlier model, it being the job of young boys and girls to stir the material with their feet sitting on a trambling board. Later mines used a round buddle stirred by a rotating arm operated by a small waterwheel.

As a small boy in the 1930s the author was given a ride on one of these, it was then derelict, part of the Golden Dagger mine. It has now gone. The only mechanical remnant of this mine is an old bogey from one of the trucks which transported material on the narrow gauge lines of the Vitifer/Golden Dagger complex.

Buddles are usually grouped in two's and three's, the material being moved from one to another to get the best purity of ore. The only known instance of settling pits being associated with a blowing house is at the right bank blowing house above Merrivale Bridge. A likely interpretation of this site is of a furnace room with wheel pit and mould by the door; to the south, stamps in a lean-to with separate wheel pit, also small mortar stone (which moves around!) and settling pits to the north. Water was drawn from a stream that comes down from Roos Tor, with offshoots to settling pits and wheels. The possibility exists that water was drawn from the Sortridge and Grimstone Leat; if so this complex was a very late tinworks.

BUDDLE, ROUND, GOLDEN DAGGER
(sx 685 799)

BOGEY, GOLDEN DAGGER

### WHEAL FREDERICK, FOXHOLES
(sx 546 854)

Tin mines, as distinct from tinners' works, are quite numerous. The author's favourite is at Foxholes beside Doe Tor Brook. Here the building is in an excellent state with launder and wheel pit, two round buddles with footsteps, all in place. Each made use of the same flow of water. There are many other interesting features round about.

# 11
# INDUSTRIAL
# STONE WORKING

Millions of years of erosion left the surface of Dartmoor covered with clitter. The inhabitants, at least from Neolithic times, utilized the debris we now refer to under the collective title 'moorstone'. Almost all the stone objects previously referred to were made of moorstone. The mason of old simply sought out a convenient rock which he then used or worked to its required shape.

It was not until the end of the eighteenth century, and beginning of the nineteenth century, that man began to extract stone from the bedrock heart of Dartmoor. It was also at this time that the method of splitting rocks changed. Previously the method used to split moorstone was to cut a series of elongated holes with the aid of a pick, then wedges were driven into the holes to cause a split. It would seem probable that iron wedges were used, but early writers refer to wooden wedges being soaked with water, the swelling giving the additional pressure to cause the rock to crack in the right direction. Some examples of this early method appear to show that a continuous groove was chipped along the line of the cut and wedges inserted at intervals. Nearly two hundred years of weathering have smoothed and rounded the edges of man's assault and examples are not easy to identify.

The new cutting method, introduced early in the nineteenth century was to drill a line of holes approximately six inches deep and six to nine inches apart. The drill was not mechanised but a solid bar with a cross-cut cutting edge was used. It must have been arm shattering on both the wielder of the hammer and holder of the bit. Once the holes were cut, two pieces of hooped iron (feathers) were inserted into the hole, between which a bar (tare) was rammed. Feather and tare, was the name by which the new method was known. The Reverend Bray, who saw this method at its introduction, likened the effect to the teeth marks of the mammoth.

Granite now became a commercial prize which could prove very profitable. The main problem to be overcome was getting the stone off the moor to points where it could easily be despatched. One answer was a horse-drawn tramway from the quarries to the nearest port. Two men, on opposite sides of the moor, tackled the job: George Templer opened his tramway from the quarries at Haytor in September 1820, and Sir Thomas Tyrwhitt opened his from the quarries at Ingra, Swell and Foggintor, in September 1823.

The Haytor Granite Tramway is a marvellous example of the use of granite and the remains for us to view are extensive. An unknown engineer devised the trackway, using the cheapest and easily the most accessible material available. The track has to rise 150 feet from Holwell Tor quarry, pass through a cutting, and then descend 1300 feet over its seven-mile length to a canal terminus. Though for most of its length it is a single track it does have sidings, a loop line, and connecting tracks to the quarry faces.

The track itself is built of roughly hewn blocks, with a carefully trimmed flange to take the flat tread wheels of the wagons. The wagons, flat topped, about thirteen feet by five feet, free-wheeled down to the canal, controlled by a primitive pole braking system. Eighteen horses were used to haul up a train of twelve wagons from Holwell Tor.

The blocks of the track vary in length, shorter lengths being used for curves, relying on the natural wear of the heavy loads to round the corners. Much larger blocks were used at points, with some form of iron lever used to physically turn the wagons in the required direction.

William White in his Gazetteer, 1850, says 'By means of this tram road and canal, immense quantities of granite are carried down to Teignmouth [by tramway to its terminus, transhipped by barge on the Stover Canal to Teignmouth] for exportation and coal, manure etc. are taken up for the use of the neighbourhood.'

It was always Sir Thomas Tyrwhitt's dream to reclaim the moorland wastes. He saw a flow of manures and fertilizers (sea sand) coming up and the enhanced agricultural produce and granite going back down the line. He never was able to achieve his aim; the Dartmoor and Plymouth Tramway was so bedevilled by financial problems that it only managed to reach the quarries, where for a time some six hundred men were employed. It was eventually extended to Princetown, being built by the owners of the quarries who carefully arranged the finance for the completion in a manner that allowed the granite to be shipped out for nothing!

Eventually the 1883 Princetown Railway overlaid most of the trackway, which in turn was absorbed by the Great Western Railway in 1922. The line was closed in 1956 and regrettably was dismantled very quickly.

For some reason these tramways were given milestones, numbers 3, 4, 5 and 6 remain in position on the Haytor Granite Tramway, the figures cut with an individual flare on a handy piece of rock. The Dartmoor and Plymouth Tramway is also marked, but only two such stones appear to remain, both on Roborough Down. On early maps the letters MS appear at intervals beside the track. These stones are smooth, circular pillars with the distance shallowly cut into the top surface.

Gunpowder, or as it was better known then as rock (a self-explanatory term), or black powder, was used at Merrivale, the firer retreating to a nearby granite shelter at the time of blasting. Not so fortunate were the miners of the Golden Dagger Mine who once on leaving their workface saw lighted fuses. They managed to dash for the exit as it exploded, without coming to much harm.

Rock powder was produced on the moor and much of the site is still there, appropriately known as Powdermills. Mr George Frean started the industry in 1844, and it lasted until the end of the century.

The three grinding-buildings, where saltpetre, sulphur and charcoal were reduced to a fine powder, were connected by a leat which was led round from building to building. In each case the water-wheel was placed centrally, the grinding stones not being granite but French burr, a mixture of clay and stone chips, made in sections and bound together by iron.

The walls of these buildings are very substantial, surviving almost intact. The roofs on the other hand were made of paper and tar, easily replaced should an accident occur. An amusing story is told of one worker who brought his lunch with him to work, eating it immediately on arrival for fear he would not survive until lunch.

Two methods of testing the powder's strength were used, one being to drill a hole in the centre of a piece of moorstone, place a known amount of powder in the hole and detonate it. This accounts for the numerous stones split by this method dotting the surrounding landscape.

The other method was to use the small mortar, which still stands beside the track down to Powdermills from the road. A known quantity of powder threw a known weight a measurable distance.

The finished product was labelled and packed in barrels for despatch. The cooper's workshop is now the shippen, while close to where the mortar stands can be found a wheel-binding stone.

Even though quarrying had become a flourishing industry, moorstone was still used in vast quantities by the owners of the Pu Tor (Pew Tor) sett. The sett enclosed not only Pu Tor but stretched north to include the Staple Tors and Roos Tor reaching toward Langstone Moor.

Under the terms of their lease, first drawn up in 1847, the contractors were not allowed to damage the heart of Pu Tor or Roos Tor, and around the centre of each tor are a set of marked stones marking the limit to which the hewers could go. On Pu Tor the marks are a circle bisected by two right angled grooves, on Roos Tor the mark is again a circle with a single bisecting line.

Nine engraved stones surround the heart of Pu Tor, and the easiest to find is a slab lying on the grass close to the top of the tor. In 1896 this area of protection was increased and four engraved stones mark the additional restricted area. These four marks differ from the original by being smaller, only six inches in diameter instead of the previous ten inch diameter. In addition they have a drilled hole at the centre and arc points.

The Duke of Bedford cannot have thought the original fourteen bounds of 1847 on Roos Tor were sufficiently clear, for in 1880 he had a post erected close to each mark. Each is engraved with the letter B.

The northern limit of the whole sett was a straight line drawn between the north-east corner of Wedlake, a moorstone with PTG1 cut on its face (recently re-erected), to another bound (PTG2) which stood on the banks of the Walkham near the Hanging Stone. This has not yet come to light.

On the south-east side of Staple Tor can be found the 'bankers' at which the cutter trimmed setts, kerb stones, and other objects from moorstone. The method was to kneel in the banker, two side stones with a rock laid across the top, while the chippings formed a mound to the front and sides. Bankers are found singly and in rows dotted around the hillside, conveniently close to the clitter being cut and trimmed.

The setts were stacked ready for transportation and a flat-topped wagon was brought onto the hillside, its rear wheels being run into trenches so that the top was at a convenient height for loading.

The cutter's tools would require constant attention, so a blacksmith's shop was built close by. This is located in Beckamoor Coombe, above the Sortridge and Grimstone Leat. Nothing much remains now except for a very fine example of a wheel-binding stone lying in front of the shop.

**MORTAR, POWDERMILLS**
(sx 628 768)

It is often said that it is strange to find an industrial site for making gunpowder in the heart of Dartmoor, even more strange to find a cannon, correctly a mortar, there as well. But what better site for such a dangerous undertaking. The mortar was used to test the powder's strength.

## CUTTING METHODS

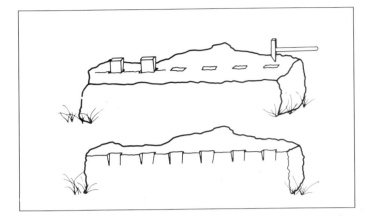 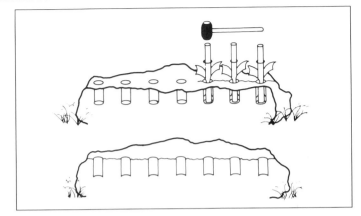

GROOVES AND WEDGE
(sx 556 686)

FEATHER AND TARE
(sx 569 695)

This example (top left) of the old method of splitting by cutting elongated holes with a pick was abandoned uncompleted. The top stones of Hawks Tor and Wind Tor also have lines of narrow holes showing where the cutter had started work.

The line of drilled holes, with jumper and hooped wedges of the feather and tare method still in position, existed for years beside a track near Burrator Reservoir. The jumper has now unfortunately been broken off.

HAYTOR QUARRIES
(sx 761 775)

Nature has a way of softening man's attack, and so it is with the Haytor Quarries. Water has formed a large pool creating a quiet oasis. As a small boy the author can remember passing this way one evening and recalls the strength and simplicity of the derrick, the crane for lifting the granite blocks, seen against the evening light. It did not eventually fall but was pushed over. More recently a small shoal of goldfish swam in the water, and a pair of kestrels reared a brood on a ledge above.

TRAMWAY IN CUTTING
(sx 759 778)

The granite track rises from Holwell Tor quarries, travels through a cutting, and past several points before descending to the Stover Canal terminus. It twists and turns to go through the southern edge of Yarner Wood to Lower Down Cross before following Stentiford Lane to Chapple. At a sharp bend it crosses the Bovey Pottery leat by the only bridge left on the track. Here the track flange becomes a groove to prevent the wheels leaving the track on the bend.

Just below the track as it passes Holwell Tor quarries is a workman's shelter. As there are plenty of buildings dotted round the sett, this small hut might have been the rock powder store, or perhaps where the operator retreated before firing the charges.

There appears to be only one bound marking the area of the sett. Dave Brewer drew my attention to the trimmed stone which is engraved with a T for Templer. On its reverse S for Somerset is cut diagonally.

POINTS
(sx 762 777)

TRACK, YARNER WOOD
(sx 780 784)

BRIDGE

GROOVED TRACK STONE
(sx 803 775)

WORKMAN'S SHELTER
(sx 752 777)

TEMPLER BOUNDSTONE
(sx 764 778)

## QUARRIES

### FOGGINTOR QUARRIES
(sx 567 736)

Sir Thomas Tyrwhitt founded the settlement at Prince's Town towards the end of the eighteenth century. Following the great movement towards land reclamation, it was Tyrwhitt's intention to turn high Dartmoor into farmland. The failure of this enterprise, and the hope of salvaging something worthwhile from his efforts, led to the establishment of the prison, to house prisoners from the Napoleonic Wars. The granite for building came from five large quarries around Foggintor, Swell Tor, Ingra Tor, and Great and Little King's Tors, the first large scale quarrying operation on the moor.

At the opening of the Dartmoor and Plymouth horse-drawn railway, in 1823, stone was soon being transported further afield. Production continued at a high rate, though not continuously, during the nineteenth century. At its height between 1830 and 1840, the quarrying here provided jobs for as many as six hundred men, and a whole community was established. Ruins of cottages, stables, a manager's house, powder house, dressing sheds, and other buildings remain at Foggintor.

FOGGINTOR RUINS
(sx x565 736)

SWELL TOR QUARRIES
(sx 560 733)

CORBELS, SWELL TOR
(sx 557 733)

In and around the many quarries on Dartmoor can be found an extraordinary array of cut and trimmed stones. Beside the track at Swell Tor quarries are a set of corbels destined for London Bridge but never used. At Little Trowlesworthy Tor is a fine example of trimming a stone in situ; this specimen was cut for a monument-base but never completed.

MONUMENT-BASE, LITTLE TROWLESWORTHY TOR
(sx 577 646)

MILESTONE 3
(sx 806 774)

MILESTONE 4
(sx 779 782)

MILESTONE 5
(sx 780 784)

MILESTONE 6
(sx 781 774)

The tramway builders erected milestones. Four survive of a possible seven on the Haytor Granite Tramway, Nos. 3, 4, 5 & 6.

Some have survived on the Dartmoor and Plymouth Tramway; these are trimmed circular pillars with the distance cut into the upper surface. They stand on Roborough Down. When this tramway was taken over by the G.W.R., the bounds of their land in Princetown followed the old tramway line to Sir Thomas Tyrwhitt's Wharf. It was marked by round iron plaques, three of which survive on the green.

G.W.R. BOUND
(sx 590 735)

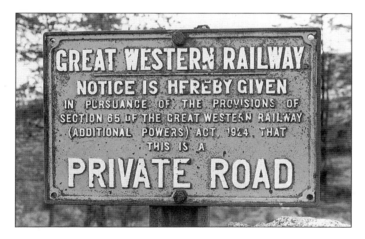

G.W.R. SIGN

For many years a sign remained to remind us that the G.W.R. did traverse
the moor, but like so many small items of nostalgia it has been broken by the
uncaring.

POWDERMILLS

POWDERMILLS, MILLHOUSE
(sx 629 772)

The walls of the milling houses are very substantial and therefore have
survived. The roofs were easily replaced if an accident occurred. The leat,
which traversed all three mills, powered water wheels set centrally athwart
the building.

290

**AERIAL VIEW OF POWDERMILLS**
(sx 629 772)

There are two tall chimneys, note the long flue to the chimney to ensure sparks were kept well clear of the explosive materials. One of the other buildings has a smart stone table, but a corner was broken off by American troops camping here in the Second World War. For years the metal debris of their occupation littered the site.

BEARING

CHIMNEY

TABLE

CRACKED TEST STONE

Apart from using the mortar to test the powder, the results of another
method of testing dot the land. Drill, charge, fire!

## PU TOR SETT

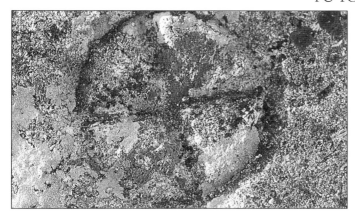

PU TOR SETT BOUND, 1847
(sx 533 735)

PU TOR SETT BOUND, 1896

ROOS TOR BOUNDSTONES
(sx 544 766)

The extraction of moorstone, the surface clitter, is an activity handed down from the first inhabitants of Dartmoor. The Pu Tor sett was the industrialization of this ample commodity. However, to prevent the destruction of the Tor an area restricting the hewers of stone was designated by markers in 1847, a circle bisected by two lines. When a new lease was issued in 1896 the area under protection was increased and its four corners were bounded by new markers, a circle bisected by two lines with additional drill holes. The centre of Roos Tor was protected in the same manner. To consolidate the bounds the Duke of Bedford had a post raised beside the old markers, engraved with the letter B.

BANKERS, STAPLE TOR
(sx 544 756)

Vast numbers of granite setts, kerbstones, etc. were cut and shaped on the
east flank of Staple Tor. The workers would kneel at a rough stone bench,
the banker, and trim the setts to size. The chippings are scattered around.
A horsedrawn wagon would be brought up to the sett makers and, for
convenience, the back wheels would be run into trenches so that the loading
could be done at a convenient height.

BANKER

WAGON TRENCHES

# 12
# EPILOGUE

The soubriquet often applied to Dartmoor, 'the last wilderness', is totally misleading. Anyone who walks over the moors, hears the tinkle of its waters, the mew of the buzzard, the croak of the raven, and the bark of the fox. The grouse shout 'go back, go back' in even the loneliest places.

A wilderness is a desert, a barren place, and that Dartmoor has never been since man first trod upon its surface.

I remember vividly parking my car at Shipley Bridge early one Spring Bank Holiday morning, scrambling up past the Naptha Works, to view China Clay dries and settling pits before walking up the Zeal Tor Tramway. Opposite the confluence of Middle Brook with the Bala Brook I turned and walked down to the stream. It was bright, sunny and windless, with a snap in the air to sharpen the senses; two cuckoos called continuously as hordes of little birds mobbed and chased them from bush to bush. Tramping up beside Middle Brook I studied the remains of the mine buildings before going on to Abb's House, the object of my walk. Abb's House was used as a stable for the Zeal Tor Tramway, which commenced operation in 1847. A stone dated GB1809 indicates an earlier operation, probably mining, as here the brook disappears into what looks like a collapsing adit.

I then walked over to Petre's Pit, disturbing two snipe, before crossing the clam. Looking down into the china clay workings I spied a fox curled up on the heather, motionless we watched each other, then to my surprise it leapt up and raced past me causing me to turn, and it ran away over the moor. Walking on a few yards I glanced up a gully on my left to see three small fox cubs playing chase around their den. Dead still, I watched them. One, two, three and they were gone. Now I knew why the fox had made me turn away.

Walking with a lilt I made my way to the tramway and back to my car, home for a late breakfast.

Wilderness, what wilderness?

I find it pleasing to report that the traditional use of 'moorstone' is still with us. The simple cross on Lake Steep to mark the passing at this spot of a local doctor, who died here of natural causes, while out walking at the beginning of the century. A cross to 'Evelyn Anthony Cave-Penney' killed in the First World War, and another cross on the Monks Path engraved SLH 1887/1965.

Other recent uses include a direction stone for the Two Moors Way and boundary stones such as those erected by the Dartmoor Preservation Association, using stone from Blackingstone Quarry. Unfortunately, the Department of the Environment used concrete posts on Long Ash Common to bound this sanctuary.

We must be for ever vigilant, and guard against the heathen, the vandal and the uncaring. But I know Dartmoor is in good hands. For four thousand or more years Beardown Man and other Dartmoor menhirs have stood in honoured memory, perhaps, of long forgotten chiefs. Sure in the knowledge that theirs too would endure forever, the people of Leusdon, in the Parish of Widecombe-in-the-Moor showed their love and respect for their chief, in a like manner. These Leusdonians marked the Silver Jubilee of their Queen, Elizabeth the Second, by taking a piece of moorstone, the very heart of their homeland, and erecting a megalith in her honour, engraved with a simple inscription

'E II R
SILVER JUBILEE
1952–1977'.

Miss Cave-Penney told me how at a meeting of all the local people her idea was taken up and the site chosen. A local farmer said there was a very fine stone in the hedge of one of his fields, another offered to move it with a tractor, and others dug the hole. It proved quite a difficult job, and caused them to ponder on the dexterity and determination of their forefathers.

The stone lay in the hedge at Primm's Hill, where there used to be a stone row, now totally obliterated, on the common nearby. It is not beyond the bounds of possibility that this stone might have been its terminal; once again it stands in honour of a chief. To me it has the right feeling about it, but then I am a Dartmoor romantic, unashamedly so.

Looking back through this collection of photographs and writings I find these words by Montaigne aptly summarize my efforts:

*I have gathered a posie*
*of other men's flowers,*
*and nothing but the thread*
*that binds them is my own.*

NATIONAL PARK SIGN
(sx 791 788)

As visitors approach the moor they are informed that they are entering the
National Park by an octagonal metal plaque fixed to a large slab of rock. Less
conspicuous is the older bound, a trimmed round head stone with the words
Dartmoor National Park set in an oval sunken panel.

NATIONAL PARK SIGN
(sx 749 693)

DARTMOOR PRESERVATION ASSOCIATION BOUND
(sx 557 704)

CROSS, LAKE STEEP
(sx 704 726)

DEPT OF ENVIRONMENT BOUND
(sx 557 750)

TWO MOORS WAY, DREWSTEIGNTON
(sx 734 908)

THE CAVE-PENNEY CROSS
(sx 684 738)

JUBILEE STONE, LEUSDON
(sx 707 732)

This final picture warms my romantic heart. We started out in just such a singular fashion with a photograph of Beardown Man, the simple standing stone, and end here at Leusdon four thousand or more years later.

# BIBLIOGRAPHY

ANONYMOUS. *An Accompt of some Mineral Observations Touching The Mines of Cornwall and Devon.* (Transactions of the Philosophical Society, 1671).

ATKINSON M, BURT R, & WAITE P. *Dartmoor Mines: The Mines of the Granite Mass. (Exeter, 1978).*

BARING–GOULD, The Rev Sabine. *A Book of Dartmoor* (London, 1923). *A Book of the West* (London, 1913). *Devonshire Characters and Strange Events.* (London, 1908).

BREWER, D. *A Field Guide to Boundary Markers on and around Dartmoor.* (Devon Books, 1982).

BORLASE, WILLIAM. *Antiquities of Cornwall.* (1769).

BROUGHTON, D.G. *The Birch Tor and Vitifer Tin Mining Complex.* (Transactions of the Cornish Institute of Engineers Vol 24).

BURT W. See Carrington N.T. *Dartmoor: A Descriptive Poem.*

BILLINGS M. *Directory of Devonshire.* (1857).

CAREW R. *The Survey of Cornwall* – F.E. Halliday, ed. (1953).

CARRINGTON N.T. *Dartmoor: a Descriptive Poem* – preface, W. Burt. (John Murray, 1826).

CROSSING, WILLIAM. *The Ancient Stone Crosses of Dartmoor.* (Exeter, 1902; republished Devon Books, 1987). *Crossing's Dartmoor Worker.* (David & Charles, 1976). *Gems in a Granite Setting.* (Plymouth, 1902; republished Devon Books, 1986). *Guide to Dartmoor* (David & Charles, 1965). *A Hundred Years on Dartmoor.* (Plymouth, 1901; republished Devon Books, 1987).

DE LA BECHE, SIR HENRY. *Report on the Geology of Cornwall, Devon and West Somerset.* (1839).

DYMOND R. *Things New and Old Concerning the Parish of Widecombe-in-the-Moor.* (1876).

EWANS M.C. *The Haytor Granite Tramway and Stover Canal.* (David & Charles, 1964).

FINBERG H.P.R. *Tavistock Abbey: A Study of the Social and Economic History of Devon.* (C.U.P., 1951).

FOX, AILEEN. *South West England.* (Thames and Hudson, 1964).

GILL, CRISPIN (Ed). *Dartmoor: A New Study.* (David & Charles, 1970).

GREEVES, T.A.P. *The Archaeology of Dartmoor from the Air.* (Devon Books, 1985). *Tin Mines and Miners of Dartmoor.* (Devon Books, 1986).

GOVER J.E.B., MAWER A., STENTON F.M. *The Place Names of Devon.* (C.U.P., 1931).

HARRIS, HELEN. *Industrial Archaeology of Dartmoor.* (David & Charles, 1968).

HARRISON. *Description of England.* (in HOLINSHED).

HOLINSHED. *Chronicles of England, Scotland and Ireland.* (6 vols, c.1600).

HEMERY, ERIC. *High Dartmoor.* (Hale, 1983).

HAYNES R.G. *Vermin Traps and Rabbit Warrens on Dartmoor.* (Post Medieaval Archaeology, Vol. 4).

KINGDOM, A.R. *The Princetown Branch.* (1979).

LEWIS, G.R. *The Stannaries: A Study of the English Tin Miner.* (Harvard, 1924).

LEWIS, W. STANLEY. *The West of England Tin Mining.* (1923).

MOOR, C.G. *Tin Mining.*

PERKINS, J.W. *Geology Explained: Dartmoor and the Tamar Valley.* (David & Charles, 1972).

PETIT, P. *Prehistoric Dartmoor*. (David & Charles, 1974).

PEVSNER, N. *The Buildings of England – South Devon*. (Penguin, 1952).

POLWHELE. *History of Devonshire*. (1973).

PRYCE, WILLIAM. *Mineralogia Cornubiensis*. (1778).

RISDON, T. *The Chorographical Description and Survey of The County of Devon*. (1811).

ROWE, The Rev, S. *A Perambulation of the Ancient and Royal Forest of Dartmoor*. (1848, republished Devon Books, 1986).

VANCOUVER, C. *General View of the Agriculture of the County of Devon*. (1808).

VOWELL, JOHN (alias J. Hooker). *Synopsis Chorographical of Devonshire*. (Blake W.J. in T.D.A. Vol 47, 1915).

WHITE, *History, Gazetteer and Directory of Devonshire*. (1850 and 1878).

WORTH, HANSFORD. *Dartmoor*. (1953, republished as *Worth's Dartmoor*, David & Charles, 1971).